# BRITAIN'S INTERNEES IN THE SECOND WORLD WAR

# BRITAIN'S INTERNEES IN THE SECOND WORLD WAR

Miriam Kochan

*First published 1983 by*
THE MACMILLAN PRESS LTD
*London and Basingstoke*
*Companies and representatives*
*throughout the world*

ISBN 0 333 28995 1

*Printed in Hong Kong*

# Contents

# List of Plates

# Preface

In 1933 the National Socialist Party came to power in Germany. Thereafter life became increasingly harsh for various sectors of the population: pacifists, liberals, Marxists, members of certain churches, gypsies, Jews, and others.

From 1933 onwards the more percipient members of these groups began to leave Germany. Slow at first, the volume of emigration grew with each fresh phase of Nazi oppression: the Nuremberg race-laws of 1935; the *Anschluss* with Austria in March 1938; *Kristallnacht*, the night of the broken glass, in November 1938 . . . .

Some 50,000 of these emigrants came to Great Britain, many intending to re-emigrate to Palestine or the United States. A large number of them were penniless, though many had once held positions of considerable importance as scientists, scholars, teachers, journalists, or had enjoyed comfortable middle-class status as doctors, dentists, lawyers, large-scale businessmen. Now they were strangers in a strange land speaking a strange language; in a word, they were refugees.

Innumerable committees sprang up in Britain to assist the settlement of the refugees, formed by, *inter alia*, the Quakers, the churches, academics and doctors. In 1933 the Central British Fund for German Jewry was founded to help the largest single group involved. In 1939 its manifold services to the refugees were carried out from Bloomsbury House, London. In 1933 too, representative leaders of the Anglo-Jewish community promised the British government that it would meet all the expenses involved in accommodating and supporting the German Jewish refugees without ultimate charge to the state.

This promise exerted some influence on the relationship between the refugees and their British hosts: there was sympathy tinged with suspicion on the one hand; gratitude tempered by insecurity on the other.

The outbreak of war between Nazi Germany and Britain in

September 1939 changed the refugee into an enemy alien and placed an unforeseen strain on the relationship (and on the promise). This book examines through the personal experiences of a few refugees the period of adjustment, with special reference to the bizarre episode of internment, until a new equilibrium was reached between Britain and its new citizens. This book would not have been written without their help.

My most grateful thanks also go to Dr David Lewis for inestimable encouragement and assistance; to Elisabeth Bender for permission to utilise the unpublished monograph by Dr Paul Jacobsthal, of which she holds the copyright; to Bernard Beecham, Gerda Hoffer and the Jewish Agency Archives in Jerusalem; to Benjy and Nicholas Kochan in London, who helped me translate German and Latin material; and to Herbert Goldsmith in London and Motty Rivlin of the Isle of Man and Netanya for pictorial material.

# The Characters in Order of Appearance

MAC GOLDSMITH. Highly successful German engineer and industrialist, he and his wife finally settled in Britain in 1937. Interned 4 September 1939; released November 1939. Now retired, after a prestigious career, in Leicester.

EDITH JACOBUS. Came to England with her husband and daughter from Germany in August 1936. Interned May 1940. She has remarried and lives in Leamington Spa.

HENRY BERG. Came to England from Germany under a Zionist youth scheme in March 1939, following a period in Dachau concentration camp. Interned July 1940. He now lives in Oxford.

PAUL JACOBSTHAL. Born 1880 in Berlin; died 1957 in Oxford, where he was a Fellow of Christ Church. Interned July 1940; released September 1940.

CHAIM RABIN. Went from Germany to Palestine and thence to England to study Hebrew and Arabic. Interned July 1940. He is now Professor of Hebrew at the Hebrew University, Jerusalem.

LEON FELDMAN. Came to England from Berlin in April 1939 on a children's transport. Interned June 1940; deported to Canada, where he was later released. He is now Professor of Hebraic Studies at Rutgers – the State University of New Jersey, and the founding rector of the Hochschule für Jüdische Studien, Heidelberg, where he is an honorary professor.

FELIX DARNBACHER. Came to England from Leipzig in 1933 as a schoolboy. Interned July 1940; deported to Australia; released in England to join the Pioneer Corps. He is now an architect living in Jerusalem.

HEINZ KIEWE. Textile journalist living in Germany, he came to London in March 1933. Interned May 1940; released February 1941. He now owns a beautiful art-needlework shop in Oxford.

PETER KATZ. Came to Britain from Germany via Holland as a

schoolboy in 1934. Interned May 1940 aged sixteen; released to
return to school in October 1940. He now lives in Oxford.

BATYA EMANUEL. Her family left Germany in the 1930s to settle in
Cardiff. Batya was still very young in 1940, but her father and
one of her brothers were interned. She now lives in Jerusalem.

JAKOB FELSENSTEIN. Frankfurt solicitor, he came to England in
April 1933. Interned July 1940; deported to Australia; released in
England in July 1941. He died in Jerusalem in 1981.

PASTOR ARNOLD EHRHARDT. Born Königsberg 1903. Studied
theology under Karl Barth in Basel after being forbidden to
lecture in the law faculty at Frankfurt University in 1935. Came
to England in July 1939; interned May 1940. He died in 1965 at
Manchester, where he was Bishop Frazer Lecturer for Church
History at the University.

MARTIN OSTWALD. Came to England from Germany via the
concentration camp of Saxenhausen, on a children's transport in
March 1939. Interned May 1940; deported to Canada, where he
was released in 1942. He is now Professor of Classics at
Swarthmore College and the University of Pennsylvania, USA.

ULRICH SKALLER. German timber-merchant, he came to England
in October 1938. Interned May 1940; released August 1940. He
now lives in retirement in Putney, London.

EUGEN GLUECKAUF. Scientist, he left Germany for England in
1933. Interned May 1940; released October 1940. He was a
Fellow of the Royal Society and worked as a consultant for the
Atomic Energy Research Establishment, Harwell, Oxon. He
died in 1981.

MOSES ABERBACH. Came to England in December 1938 on a
children's transport. Interned May 1940; released July 1940. He
is now a professor at the Baltimore Hebrew College, USA.

KURT AND FREDA. Escaped from Germany via Holland in May
1940. Immediately interned; released August 1942. They now
live in Leicester.

MARIE NEURATH. Escaped with fiancé Otto Neurath on the same
boat as Kurt and Freda and interned on arrival. Released in
February 1941. She is now widowed and lives in London.

DR H. A doctor in a Vienna hospital, she came to England on a
domestic permit via Denmark in 1938. Interned May 1940. She
now lives in London.

KLAUS LOEWALD. Came from Berlin to England. Interned June
1940; deported to Australia, where he was released to join the

Australian Army in August 1942. He now teaches history at the University of New England, Armidale, New South Wales.

JULIUS CARLEBACH. Left Hamburg in December 1938 and came on a children's transport to England. Interned June 1940; released October 1940. He now teaches sociology at the University of Sussex.

ERNST MANASSE. Came to England from Germany on a Zionist youth scheme in March 1939 after a sojourn in Dachau concentration camp. Interned July 1940; released October 1940. He is now retired and lives in Oxford.

RUDI GUTTMAN. Sent to school in England from Germany in 1934. Interned July 1940; deported to Australia; released in Britain early in 1941 to join the Pioneer Corps. Now an engineer living in Tel Aviv.

ERICH MARK. Came to England from Germany as a young boy. Interned June 1940; released October 1940. Now lives in Belgium.

HENRY PRAIS. Came to Britain in 1939 with a Zionist youth group on an agricultural permit. Interned July 1940; released December 1940. Now a retired Professor of French living in Jerusalem.

Scale 1 : 5,000,000

Lochgilphead
Strachur
Glasgow
Liverpool
Bury
Manchester
Huyton
Prees Heath
Sutton Coldfield
Clacton-on-Sea
London
Kempton Park
Lingfield
Seaton
Paignton

MAP I  Map showing the sites of the internment-camps in Great Britain

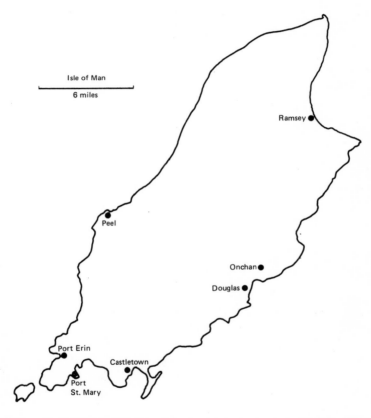

Isle of Man

6 miles

Ramsey

Peel

Onchan

Douglas

Port Erin

Castletown

Port
St. Mary

MAP 2    Map showing the sites of the internment-camps on the Isle of Man

# 1 The Sheep and the Goats

On 3 September 1939 Great Britain declared war on Nazi Germany. As a consequence some 70,000 Germans and Austrians then living in the country became enemy aliens. The following day in the House of Commons, Arthur Greenwood, Deputy Leader of the Opposition, asked the Secretary of State for the Home Department what steps he intended to take to deal with these aliens in time of war.

His question did not catch Sir John Anderson unprepared. The problem was not a new one. In the First World War, Britain had at various periods pursued an active policy of rounding up and confining, in camps throughout the country, the nationals of the countries she was fighting, partly on the assumption that a man must be presumed to owe his first allegiance to the land of his birth and that consequently his presence at large would endanger the British war effort; partly on the grounds that his own safety might be jeopardised by British wartime xenophobia.

In 1914–18 the process of internment had encountered numerous difficulties. The number of enemy aliens in the country was not known and the provision of suitable accommodation with reasonable living conditions had been hazardous in the extreme. In addition, the release of competent manpower to run the camps and ensure security had been considered undesirable. So great had been the problems involved that in 1923 the Committee of Imperial Defence had decided that the best policy to pursue towards enemy aliens in times of future war would be to expel them.

The situation in 1939 was very different. The solution of expulsion had been rendered impracticable and the question of loyalty was no longer so simple. Of the 70,000-odd enemy aliens resident in Britain at that date, some 55,000 were refugees from Hitler's Nazi regime in Germany and German-dominated Austria. Large numbers had been deprived of their nationality and become stateless persons. Thousands had already been imprisoned in German concentration camps. For nearly all, return, even if possible, would have meant certain suffering and probable death.

By September 1939 these people, a large proportion of them Jews, victims of Nazi racialism, had found asylum on British soil and were slowly, painfully rebuilding from scratch the lives Hitler had ruined. Their hatred of the Nazi regime had deeper roots and stronger foundations than any emotion a citizen of the United Kingdom might be expected to experience.

Finally, the enemy alien was no longer an unknown factor. Since 1919 strict control had been exercised over immigration into Britain. The whereabouts, occupation and character of every alien resident were theoretically known to the police. He had to report to his local police station within three months of his arrival in the country, there to receive the indispensable 'registration book'; if he changed his residence, he was obliged to report to the police in the new district within forty-eight hours.

The British government therefore, when framing its policy towards its enemy aliens in 1939, decided against general internment and opted instead for a dual plan. 'Effective steps must be taken', Sir John told the House, 'to render harmless all aliens who may be hostile to this country . . . but there should be no unnecessary interference with other foreigners of whom many are anxious to help this country.' In Arthur Greenwood's words, there would be 'a sharp distinction between those who are the victims of the system we are now fighting, and those who may be properly under suspicion'.

The *Jewish Chronicle*, organ of British Jewry, welcomed this pronouncement. 'The words of Sir John Anderson . . . must have lifted a load of anxiety from the minds of many refugees', it concluded on 8 September. 'It will have confirmed the belief which they of all people must have been brought to hold, that Britain shows indeed a shining example of humanity in a world where inhumanity has threatened civilisation with a new night of barbarism . . . every refugee with a clear conscience will be filled with gratitude for this splendid treatment.'

Meanwhile, the German Jewish Aid Committee, centred at Bloomsbury House, London, issued instructions to the refugees to assist them to be worthy of 'splendid treatment'. They were, among other things, to avoid talking German in public, and to obey honourably all directions of the police.

But how to differentiate between one category and the other – while maintaining due concern for the security of the realm? As early as August 1939 a Foreign Office minute noted that 'difficulties might arise in distinguishing the sheep from the goats'. What was Sir John Anderson's solution to this very real problem?

In the first place, he was able to report on 4 September that certain security measures had already been taken: a number of aliens 'whose suspicious activities' had been under observation were already under detention. Internment of enemy aliens in this, and all future cases during the war, took place under the royal prerogative.

Secondly, an Order in Council had been made amending the peacetime Aliens Order so that all enemy aliens who did not intend to leave the country immediately were required to report to the police. They had to obtain police permits if they wished to change their residence, travel, or own certain articles such as cameras or motor-cars.

Lastly, the information already available had to be supplemented to make it possible to sift out any person who, though claiming to be a refugee, might not in fact be friendly to Britain. To this end, Sir John announced, there would be an immediate review of all Germans and Austrians in Britain. He had asked a number of men with legal experience to assist him, and these examiners would sit in tribunals in London and the provinces to examine all cases and consider who could properly be left at large, who interned, who subjected to other restrictions.

But what of those aliens for whom this meticulous procedure was felt to be unnecessary, those specifically who, on 4 September, Sir John had been able to report as already in detention? By summer 1938 the head of MI5, Sir Vernon Kell, had compiled a list of persons suspected of being obvious dangers to the state. Even before war was declared, the British police, armed with this list, had swooped. They had instructions to convey those they arrested to the nearest police station, thence to the nearest internment camp.

Altogether some 415 enemy aliens were arrested in this first onslaught. They included Eugen Spier, a German Jew who had come to Britain in 1922, and who described his experiences in a book, *The Protecting Power*. Also on the list was German Jewish industrialist Mac Goldsmith. Already highly successful in Germany, manufacturing valuable components, Goldsmith had been positively welcomed to England in 1937. By the outbreak of war the factories he had opened in Leicester and Welwyn Garden

City had finally begun to make money, after an uphill struggle. In July 1939 Goldsmith, with foresight, moved his family from London to a house in Clifton, near Deddington, Oxfordshire.

'As soon as war was declared,' he told me, 'instructions came that aliens could not travel more than five miles, so I could not go to my factory. I was sitting in our garden when the policeman from the next village came. He said, "I am awfully sorry, but I have instructions from the Chief Constable of Banbury to take you in." He was most apologetic. I told my wife I had to go to a hearing, as I did not want her to know yet that I was going to be interned. So I packed an overnight case, and we went to the Chief Constable, who was very friendly. He said, "I am very sorry for this, but orders are orders. I have two refugee children in my own house." He took me for a cup of tea, and waited for instructions from the London headquarters. Finally, he received a call from Scotland Yard, and I was to be taken to Oxford prison. I stopped at Deddington on the way and asked the policeman to look after my family. I heard later that he went over every day while I was away to see them.

'Then we arrived in Oxford and the big prison-doors opened. By then I was as hungry as a lion; it was about 9 p.m. I had to wait for the doctor to examine me. The doctor was a most undesirable character and we soon had some arguments, as he obviously considered me an enemy alien. I told the prison staff that I was terribly hungry and that I had had nothing to eat since lunch-time. They brought me cocoa with beads of fat on the top. I said, "I am not drinking that." The bread and margarine I had.

'After they had taken everything away from me so I could not commit suicide, they put me into a cell and I had a good night's sleep as I was completely exhausted. At 6 a.m. my door was opened and the warden said, "Empty your slops." I said, "What is that?" I had never heard that word before. Then they brought a bowl of soup. I said, "I am sorry, I cannot eat that; I shall have to have vegetarian food." I got something to eat eventually – they brought me a bowl of porridge.

'I asked to see the governor. There was a long queue, mostly prisoners from Wormwood Scrubs who had been evacuated and brought to Oxford for security reasons. The language was atrocious. When I finally got into his office, I asked him whether I could get kosher food [conforming to the Jewish dietary laws], and he said, "No." I told him that I would have to have vegetarian food. The food was brought in from a pub nearby.

'My cell neighbour came in and asked me what I was in for. I said I did not know. When I asked him the same question, he said he had swindled a few people. He was a South African Jew. Then I went to the library, and I still remember that I borrowed *Disraeli* by André Maurois. In the afternoon, there was a knock at my door and the prison visitor came in and introduced himself as a Mr Henriques, a most charming and cultured man. We found we knew so many people. Then I asked him if he could do me a great favour, "Could you ring up my wife and tell her I need underwear?" "We're not supposed to do that", he said. "I am not asking you to do anything politically risky", I replied. He obliged, and rang up without giving his name. Next day, our nanny came with my things. Twice a day we had exercise and a cigarette. I threw my stubs away. They told me not to do that because they traded in the stubs.

'After a few days, they said that perhaps I would like to be with the other internees. I said I did not mind. They were non-Jews. It was their biggest astonishment when I laid *tephillim* [phylacteries]; they were quiet and respectful. There were Nazis there too.'

The presence of 'Nazis', a recurrent source of comment and complaint on the part of the Jewish internees throughout their captivity, is not surprising at this period in view of the composition of the inhabitants of the camps. The 337 enemy aliens whom Osbert Peake, Under-Secretary for the Home Office, reported as confined in six camps on 11 October 1939 included persons who had been resident in Britain at the outbreak of war, enemy nationals who had arrived at ports after that date, and the crews of captured German merchant ships, such as the *Pomona*, caught in the London docks when war broke out. A week later, Sir Vernon Warrender, Secretary of State for War, put the figure at 660, all at that juncture concentrated in three camps.

It should be noted that right from the beginning the cumbersome mechanism was in force whereby male enemy aliens arrested by the police on the instructions of the Home Office were handed over to the military authorities for custody. In other words, there was a division of responsibility: the Home Office decided government internment policy; the War Office arranged the custody of the interned.

Not surprisingly, in view of the few camps in use, Spier and Goldsmith followed a similar itinerary. Spier was arrested and taken to Olympia on 1 September. He claims to have been registered as prisoner of war no. 2, second to Baron Constant von

Pillar. He was taken through a line of soldiers with fixed bayonets into a vast empty hall furnished only with a table and two wooden benches and occupied solely by two British intelligence officers. The dominant impression was of unpreparedness: the sleeping-quarters on the first floor of the building, consisting of wooden three-tiered bunks, were not yet equipped with bedding; no arrangements had been made for breakfast on the first day; the building was in semi-darkness because of blackout regulations. By the second morning most of these deficiencies had been made good (a breakfast of tea, bread and margarine was served) and arrangements for the election of a camp leader to liaise between the prisoners and the camp commandant had been made, giving rise to the inevitable pro- and anti-Nazi disputes. But by then Spier had been moved on. Goldsmith, on the other hand, had arrived.

'One day the order came that we were taking off from Oxford – no one knew where to. We were handcuffed; I protested, "I'm not a criminal!" We were taken to Olympia. I was delivered against a receipt. The officers who received us looked at the handcuffs because all the other internees from other prisons were brought in without handcuffs. Then it was *Rosh Hashanah* [ the Jewish New Year; in 1939 it fell on 14 September]. I said, "Why can't we have a rabbi, why can't we have a service?" But nothing was organised, as always in England.'

Spier was at Butlin's Holiday Camp at Clacton-on-Sea for the High Holy Days. His request for permission to attend synagogue or to have a room allotted for worship was refused, but he was allowed to refrain from food on 23 September 1939, the Jewish Day of Atonement, a twenty-five hour fast. On the other hand, the living conditions were surprisingly good: two men were assigned to each chalet, supplied with two extremely comfortable bunks and plenty of white woollen blankets, wardrobe, mirror and hot and cold running water. The food was good if inadequate. The idyll was only marred by the barbed wire which separated the chalets from the outside world, so that the prisoners had to be marched to the dining-room by guards with bayonets. As autumn advanced their well-worn path became a swamp, ankle-deep in mud. Again, we find the problems of Nazis versus anti-Nazis arising from the election of a camp-leader, and also complaints of the late arrival of food-parcels.

Goldsmith must have arrived at Butlin's when the honeymoon period was over: 'It was quite all right except that they had taken Nazis there – prisoners from German merchant ships. On the first night they put me together with a homosexual – but in the same bed because there was only one bed. But he did not make any attempts. We were treated very well. There was a man called Schiffer, who was a Gestapo man, in England with his wife and girlfriend (she was a daughter of Bechstein). Schiffer always pretended that he was a Nazi originally, but no longer. But he was a spy. MI5 treated him very well until Christmas, when he got drunk and said, "God punish England." And then they got him. Also here was Hitler's best friend, Putzi Hanfstaengl, who had been sent off by the Nazis to Switzerland on a mission. He had got away and come to England. This was the sort of company we had there. There was also the Czech Jewish editor of a newspaper, Dr Winter, a very nice chap.'

In mid October the internees at Clacton were officially informed that they were being moved *en masse* to Seaton in Devon. However, an element of choice was surprisingly introduced: if they were prepared to pay 4s 6d a day they could obtain better conditions at Paignton. Most, including Spier, opted for Seaton. Mac Goldsmith went to Paignton, 'where we were treated very well by a man who had himself been interned in Germany in the First World War. He said, "If you behave yourselves, you will be treated well." However, we could not have any visitors.'

It had not been envisaged that the disparate body of 'suspicious' people whose arrest had taken place so precipitously at the outbreak of war should be deprived of the right to appeal. On 4 September, Sir John Anderson announced his intention of setting up an advisory committee to hear any representations from internees and to advise the Secretary of State as to whether they could properly be released. The chairman of this committee was Sir Walter Monckton. Its members were Sir Arthur Hazlerigg, Professor W. E. Collinson and J. J. Mallon, with G. P. Churchill as secretary. By October, however, it was thought advisable to expedite proceedings and a second panel was established, this time under the chairmanship of Norman Birkett. It was before this second panel that Goldsmith appeared.

'Finally, we were taken to the Oratory School in Brompton Road, London. By then, they were ready for the hearings. I made friends with a number of people. One of them was the chief engineer of an aircraft firm; he designed bombers here. Another was a director of Siemens. We were in bunks there and had a wonderful time telling stories, while the soldiers who watched over us got us beer. My wife got permission to visit me there. There was a Jewish captain in charge. My wife brought challahs [plaited loaves] for *Shabbat* [the Sabbath]; he could not believe that she was Jewish. The captain and I found we had friends in common.

'I was interviewed by an MI5 man. He apologised that it had taken so long but "we are not organised for this sort of thing in England". He asked me how I got my money out. I said I would rather not say. "Have you had any news from your wife?" I said, "No, I am rather worried. She is coming before a tribunal today." At that moment, a soldier came into the room and whispered in his ear. He turned to me and said, "You do not have to worry." Then he told me the reason I was interned: I had been cleared by all the services except the Admiralty.

'Then I was called before the Home Secretary's Advisory Committee. A great English judge, Sir Norman Birkett, was the chairman of the committee, which consisted of the first woman minister, Margaret Bondfield, and a lot of very eminent people. They asked me questions; they had all my files, letters, references, etc. I said that I had been treated well except for being handcuffed. They were very shocked. It was marvellous, that hearing, absolutely marvellous. It was a most friendly atmosphere. I could have cried. Where in the world would they treat an enemy alien like that? After one and a half hours of thorough questioning, they asked me if I had any questions to ask. I said, "After being interned, my friends will think there is something wrong with me." They said, "Don't worry: we are not like that in England."

'So I was taken back to camp and next morning at nine o'clock the commanding officer called me in. He said, "You had your hearing yesterday afternoon; you were back at five or six o'clock. You must know how to pull strings!" I said, "What do you mean?" He replied, "I have just received a message from the Home Office to say that you must be released immediately. Normally, it takes three or four weeks."

'So I came home one *Shabbat* afternoon to my mother's house. On Tuesday, I was in Leicester in my office. I was allowed to use my car, and I used to go to the aircraft-factories. I was given a pass to go into any establishment I wanted. I was left completely alone in May 1940. I had stamped on my identity card "Not to be interned".'

At this point his wife joined in the conversation, saying, 'He had no restrictions. I had restrictions. I had to observe the curfew. I had to be in at 10.15 p.m. He was head of the fire-watchers. On New Year's Eve, I had to go to the police to ask permission to be out late;

I was allowed to stay out till midnight! They took my bicycle away. When he was interned I was not allowed to exceed the five-mile limit.'

Mac went on, 'I could travel anywhere. I was working with the authorities all the time. I used to go to Rolls-Royce regularly and one day I was going in with a colonel from a tank establishment. I showed my pass and walked straight in. They called the colonel in to show his credentials! I said, "This world is crazy. I should be the English colonel. You should be the German Jewish refugee!"'

Eugen Spier, who appeared before the panel of the Advisory Committee chaired by Sir Walter Monckton was not so fortunate. His reaction to the experience was diametrically opposed to Goldsmith's. Face to face with the committee, he writes, 'I became more than at any time before conscious of the fact that I was actually a prisoner under arrest and that I was now to face a trial without any legal assistance for my defence.' Later he concludes, 'Apparently the words "foreigner" and "foe" were still synonymous in the eyes of the majority of the members of this tribunal.'

In November 1939 Spier was taken to a new camp at Lingfield racecourse to continue his career as an internee.

By 23 November the Advisory Committees had dealt with ninety-two cases.

# 2 The Greatest Possible Expedition

Meanwhile no time had been wasted in embarking on the formidable task of separating sheep from goats. By 28 September 1939 the tribunals, headed by men of legal experience, had begun to work their way through an examination of every enemy alien over the age of sixteen registered in Britain, with the object of sifting out anyone who, though claiming to be a refugee, might not in actuality be friendly to the country.

Some 120 tribunals were established, assigned to different areas throughout the country. As speed was the order of the day, no one tribunal was supposed to deal with more than 500 cases. In districts of London where large numbers of Germans and Austrians congregated, several tribunals were set up. There were, for example, eleven in North-West London, a great centre of refugee life, and four each in South, East and West London. Responsibility for arranging for the particulars of each individual case to be available to the tribunal lay with the police.

Representatives of the police and also of the service intelligence departments had been consulted when the Home Office drew up the instructions containing advice and guidance on the principles chairmen of tribunals should follow when examining the cases before them. They were reminded that 'Germans and Austrians in this country, being nationals of a state with which His Majesty is at war, are liable to be interned as "enemy aliens" but most of the Germans and Austrians now here are refugees from the regime against which this country is fighting, and many of them are anxious to help the country which has given them asylum. . . . It would therefore be wrong to treat all Germans and Austrians as though they were "enemies".'

The main brief of the tribunals was to divide the enemy aliens into three categories: 'A', to be interned; 'B', exempt from internment but subject to the restrictions decreed by the Special Order; and 'C', exempt from both internment and restrictions. They also had to make the supplementary decision whether the individual should be classified as 'a refugee from Nazi oppression' or placed in a class of 'non-refugees'. Their findings were stamped on the alien's registration card.

The need for speed, it was claimed, dictated the injunction that aliens appearing before the tribunals could not be represented by a solicitor or barrister, and also that hearings were held in private. 'It is desired', said Sir John, 'to complete the review with the greatest possible expedition. This object would not be attained if every case had to be dealt with as though the alien were being tried in a court of law.' The alien could, however, bring a friend or a witness who might be helpful to his case. Aliens were also advised if possible to bring testimonials from their employers and also character references from people of responsibility who had known them for a number of years. In addition, arrangements had been made for the Refugee Joint Consultative Committee to send an accredited representative to each tribunal.

The sense of urgency was obviously communicated to the legal gentlemen. Mrs Jacobus's husband, 'like all refugees, was called to a tribunal. They asked him what he was doing. He said he was the representative of such and such a firm and he had the permission of the Home Office to do this. But a mistake had been made: it was not entered in his little grey book. The man said that, as it was not written in, he had to stamp it "Enemy Alien". My husband said that he could go and get papers to prove that he had permission. But the man said, "No time!" and stamped the book "B".'

By 28 October the tribunals had dealt with 13,031 cases and classified 9656 of them as 'C', 3189 as 'B' and interned 186.

First reaction to the tribunals was favourable. 'Those aliens to whom I have spoken', wrote the *Jewish Chronicle*'s special correspondent on 27 October, 'have been filled with nothing but praise for the kind way in which they have been treated. One or two judges in particular, have been most highly lauded for their gentleness and understanding. Aliens have been asked, among many other things, why they left Germany, what their attitude to Hitler is, and whether they would be willing to work for this country.'

And certainly many of the enemy aliens, particularly those graded 'C', found the tribunals and those that manned them not unpleasant.

'I'd been to a tribunal in Bedfordshire', Henry Berg told me. 'It was very hail-fellow-well-met: "I trust you are well! How do you like it in this country?" The tribunal was casual as far as I was concerned. "The holder of this card is to be exempted until further order from internment and from the special restrictions applicable to enemy aliens under the Aliens Order 1920 as amended. Refugee from Nazi oppression (24–10–39)." There appeared to be a file on me: they told me who I was.'

'It is an honour for this country to have you', the chairman of his tribunal told Paul Jacobsthal.

Even Chaim Rabin found something kind to say, though sorely tried: 'I was living in Willesden Green when war broke out. I was called to a tribunal. There I said, "I have come because I have been invited, but I have no reason to be here. I have nothing to do with this", and I showed them a letter I had received from the German Embassy in London in 1939 saying that I had lost my nationality and asking me to return my passport. (I didn't.) They said, "Sorry, we do not recognise illegal acts." I was put in category "C".
. . . The people at the tribunal looked like ex-army people or civil servants. They were very nice and talked to me extremely nicely.' In fact on the first day of the war Sir John Anderson had specifically stated that 'Refugees from Germany and Austria who were nationals of those countries, are registered as either German or Austrian and must therefore be so classified . . . notwithstanding that they may have been deprived of German nationality by some German law.'

Leon Feldman had a variation on the same problem: 'I was born in Berlin', he says. 'We were never German citizens; we were always stateless. My father came from a place in Galicia that later became part of the USSR. The Russians offered him an Ukrainian passport but he refused. I was born in 1921 and, after a minimum of ten years residence in Germany, neither my father nor I, who attended public school and gymnasium in Berlin, did qualify for German naturalisation because of the changing political situation which prevailed in the early 1930s. At the outbreak of war I went before a tribunal. The man there was a kind of bland-type official, with a ruddy complexion and a big imperial moustache. He told me that he had been in the imperial service; now he was an interrogating officer. I told him I was stateless. He said, "You're a German." I said, "No." He declared me a friendly alien of technically enemy nationality. I told him I had been expelled from Germany. That "technically

enemy alien" irked me more than anything else. They applied their
own criterion that was totally inapplicable to a Jew from Germany.
I tried to explain. He said he knew, he understood. But it just didn't
penetrate.'

True to form, a wealth of Jewish humour grew up around
tribunal experiences. The *Jewish Chronicle* printed an example on
9 February:

> A young German rabbi appearing before an Aliens Tribunal was
> asked whether he was Orthodox or Liberal. He replied that he
> was a minister of a Liberal congregation in Germany but he
> supposed he would be regarded as Orthodox here. 'Well, do you
> keep the dietary laws?' enquired the Chairman. 'Yes, I keep
> them, though not very strictly', replied the applicant. The
> Chairman: 'Please be a little more specific in your replies. Do you
> eat oysters, for instance?' The Rabbi: 'No: I don't eat oysters.'
> The Chairman after a pause: 'Then you have no idea what you
> miss.'

Felix Darnbacher also remembers his tribunal with a degree of
amusement, 'There was a major there, with a lady beside him.
"What are you doing?" the man asked. "I go to school", I said, and
I showed him some marks I had got from the Polytechnic. "Here",
he said, "it says 'could do better'!" We all got "C". My father was
vouched for by the British Legion.'

But doubts as to the uniform standard of the decisions reached by
the 120 legal gentlemen were coming to the surface as early as
November 1939. 'Is the Home Secretary aware', asked Geoffrey le
Mesurier Mander, MP for Wolverhampton, East, 'that there has
been a good deal of variation in treatment by the large body of
tribunals throughout the country?'

The aliens themselves were all too aware of this fact: 'I went to the
tribunal', one refugee said, 'and he asked me "Have you any
relations in Germany?" I said, "Yes". So I was graded "B".'

Heinz Kiewe came to England shortly after Hitler came to power
in 1933. 'I was an emigrant and not a refugee and my family was
declared as being German emigrants by an Ealing judge: category
"B".'

Peter Katz was more or less right in his assessment of the situation.
'Aliens were classified into three groups. "A", considered a danger
to the country. This was quite often haphazard. They were refugees
like us but they were interned immediately. Quite a few were later

released. "B", not considered dangerous enough to be interned immediately. "C", friendly enemy aliens, refugees from Nazi oppression. The great bulk were these – except in certain areas. It depended on the whim of the chairman of the tribunal. In camp people used to say, "Where are you from? Oh, yes, that was a tough area." '

Cardiff, where the Emanuel family lived, must have been one such 'tough area'. Batya Emanuel told me, 'I hadn't been through a tribunal because I was under sixteen, but my family had. There was a horrible little man there who had made everyone "A" or "B", but it seems he got it in the head because everyone was asked to come again, and this time my parents and brothers were made "C".'

Concern at these obvious discrepancies in assessment very quickly led the Home Office to issue supplementary instructions to the aliens tribunals on 21 October. Henceforth Germans and Austrians coming before a tribunal should be placed in one of only two categories. In the first would be those who were found to be well disposed to Britain and unlikely to do anything to assist the enemy or hinder the national war effort. This category, the instructions specified, would include large numbers of refugees and other persons who had ties of association or sympathy with Britain. People in this category would be exempt from restrictions unless there were special reasons to keep them restricted.

The second category would embrace Germans and Austrians who were not refugees and who had no firm ties of association or sympathy with Britain. They would remain subject to the restrictions – if they were not interned.

But who actually was a refugee? Obviously the tribunals were not too clear about the interpretation of the term. There was, for example, a case cited in the *Jewish Chronicle* of 3 November 1939 of an enemy alien who was asked by the Wealdstone, Middlesex, tribunal whether he had been arrested by the Gestapo. 'No', replied the alien. He was a Jew who had been ordered by the Gestapo to leave the country. 'Does not wish to be repatriated. Not a refugee from Nazi oppression', wrote the chairman on his registration book.

It had never been intended, the supplementary instructions stated, to limit the definition of a refugee to someone who had been interned in a concentration camp or subjected to actual physical ill-treatment. A refugee was anyone who had been prevented from carrying on his profession or occupation or earning his living and was deprived of the protection of his government.

The instructions also noted that some doubtful cases had arisen of people who had left Germany and Austria some years earlier and had therefore not themselves been subjected to actual oppression. In this event, it was left to the tribunals to decide, on the basis of the information available, whether the alien had had reasonable grounds for anticipating oppressive treatment and whether it had been on these grounds that he had come to Britain.

'The instructions should practically exempt all loyal refugees in this country from restrictions', rejoiced the *Jewish Chronicle* on 3 November.

There were, however, other problems. The difficulty of communication between German-speaking alien and very English tribunal was raised in the House of Lords in November, when Earl de la Warr, President of the Board of Education, was able to announce that it had been arranged for interpreters to be available for all tribunals.

But other causes for disquiet remained. Jakob Felsenstein tells the story of 'a man on the *Arandora Star* who nearly lost his life because a German-born relative wrote an unfavourable letter to his tribunal saying "that man can not be trusted" – and it was about a financial matter, too, nothing to do with loyalty. When the tribunal asked him about the money in question, he said, "What has that to do with my loyalty?" The judge said, "I am the one who asks the questions here." He was given "A" and immediately interned.'

'There was a German Jewish nurse in Cardiff who worked in a hospital and who typed letters to her mother in German', Batya Emanuel tells. 'Some of the nurses heard her typing and asked "Why should a nurse type?" She was made "A" and was interned immediately.'

Is the implication here that the nurses passed on their doubts to the tribunal? Where, in fact, did the tribunals get their information? The fear of 'secret' information being laid to their discredit haunted every refugee in wartime Britain, a legacy perhaps of the evil days in Nazi Germany. The Home Secretary did little to allay their anxiety. Asked in the House on 26 October whether the tribunals were permitted to receive evidence of an anonymous character against alien refugees; whether the refugees were informed of it and of its source, and whether they could be interned on the basis of it without the opportunity to rebut it, Sir John could only reply that it was open to the tribunals to consider any evidence which might be placed before them. However, he was satisfied that, given the composition of the tribunals, their decisions would not be influenced by untested evidence of an anonymous nature.

His confidence was not shared. Doubts as to the validity of the tribunals' judgements sounded loud and clear. They even reached the House of Lords, where in early November Lord Newton voiced strong suspicions that a certain number of enemy aliens had been interned who were perfectly harmless and innocent. He knew a young German writer . . . . On the other side of the fence, in the other House, but also on 2 November, Colonel Nathan (MP for Central Wandsworth) asked the Home Secretary whether representations which might be made to him about those who had been certified 'B' or 'C' but ought, it was felt, to have been certified 'A' would be available to the tribunals.

Sir John could only reaffirm his faith in the reliability of his tribunals. 'My impression is that they have exercised their discretion with great care.' 'It is not contemplated', he said on 23 November, 'that as regards all or most of these cases, a further examination by the Advisory Committees shall be undertaken.' But the decisions of the tribunals were not irrevocable. In any case where the police or the service intelligence departments could give him information which suggested that a case required further consideration, the decision of the tribunal would be reviewed in its light. It was equally open to review on behalf of the alien concerned.

Aliens who were actually interned did, as we have seen, have the right of appeal to the Advisory Committees. By 1 February they had dealt with 162 cases and granted release in forty-five, after consideration of their reports. That the wheels of these committees ground slowly was open to no doubt. 'Would the Minister agree', ran a question in the Commons on 17 January 1940, 'that an appeal which has been in for three and a half months to the Appeals Tribunal and had not yet been considered is a little overdue?'

It was in the murky area of the 'Bs', created by the early tribunals, that the clamour for review was loudest. People placed in this category, it should be recalled, were exempted from internment but not from the special restrictions, because, in the view of the tribunals, their friendliness to Britain was not so clearly demonstrated that they could properly be freed from these requirements.

By the second half of November 1939 the government at last seemed prepared to respond to the numerous appeals to utilise the services of the refugees. They were permitted to enlist in certain branches of the armed services (November) and to take employment (December) if they had been cleared by a tribunal. To accelerate this process, four new tribunals were established in North-West London. At this juncture 35,000 cases altogether had been reviewed and 348 people interned.

The new freedom could not but highlight the position of the unfortunate 'Bs'. Hampered by the travel restrictions, not allowed to register with a labour exchange, carrying the stigma of being found wanting, their chances of obtaining employment were small – though they were permitted to work if they could find a job themselves within five miles of their home. Members of the Parliamentary Committee on Refugees – Major Cazalet, Eleanor Rathbone, David Grenfell and T. E. Harvey – accompanied by representatives of the Central Refugee Committee, placed these arguments before Osbert Peake, and asked that 'Bs' should be given the same right to appeal against the tribunals' decisions as was enjoyed by the interned enemy aliens in category 'A'.

In January 1940 Sir John Anderson announced that he was considering a scheme for a further review of their cases.

# 3 The Enemy Within

By the middle of February 1940 Osbert Peake could tell the House of Commons that nearly all the tribunals had completed their work. They had examined over 70,000 cases out of a total of 74,000 registered Germans and Austrians. All had been classed 'C', except 528 cases when internment orders had been made, and 8000 cases where the tribunals had decided not to grant exemption from the special restrictions applicable to enemy aliens.

At the end of the month, the substance of Sir John's scheme for a review of the tribunals' decisions was known. Twelve Advisory Committees were to be set up, one in each of the central towns of the Civil Defence regions, and three in London. Each committee would be composed of a chairman with legal qualifications (in the event, they were all KCs) and a panel of lay members who were prominent residents in their regions. The Committee when it sat would consist of the chairman and two lay members drawn from the panel. In addition, the chairman would be assisted by two representatives of the Defence Department when the Committee was considering the cases of aliens resident in the protected area.

On 21 March the details of the functions of these committees were announced. Their task had been expanded. Not only were they to undertake the review originally announced of Germans and Austrians who had been placed in the intermediate 'B' category, they were also to review cases where, as a result of fresh information or for some other special reason, the police had grounds for thinking that reclassification of 'C' grades was desirable. In addition, the Committees were asked to undertake an examination of cases of aliens of all nationalities residing in or around certain important naval centres.

The *Jewish Chronicle*'s first instinct was to reassure: unofficial sources, its special correspondent reported soothingly on 29 March, 'state that only the "bad eggs" in the "C" category will come under review'. Even as the unpleasant truth gradually dawned, the

*Chronicle* remained calm. 'This is, no doubt, a step taken in the interests of national security', it regretfully concluded on 5 April. 'The inquiry will probably be welcomed, despite its irksomeness, by all genuine refugees, if only as a means of allaying what are too often sedulously fostered fears and suspicions. And even such a departure from British practice as that which stipulates that any case of doubt must be resolved not in favour of the accused but in favour of the safety of the country will be appreciated in the light of the present tragic circumstances.'

It could only hope that the chairmen of the new committees had been chosen for their complete impartiality and ability to form wise and independent judgements which could not be swayed by the unintelligent 'hue and cry of the sensational press who would like to "intern the lot" '.

And, indeed, mounting xenophobia was percolating into the country. Articles in the *Daily Sketch* and the *Sunday Express* late in January 1940 gave body to a fear that all refugees were spies. On 2 March, Sir John Anderson wrote to his father, 'The newspapers are working up feeling about aliens. I shall have to do something about it or we may be stampeded into an unnecessarily offensive policy. It is very easy in wartime to start a scare.' Late in March, Colonel Henry Walter Burton, MP for Sudbury, West Suffolk, gave an interview to the press. 'In the main', he was quoted as saying, 'these aliens are supposed to be refugees but nobody knows how many spies have come over with the refugees. You cannot take these risks in wartime. There are 74,000 enemy aliens at large, and people round the coast are very apprehensive.

'I would have all enemy aliens over fourteen interned. I think eventually that will have to come. At present enemy aliens are going about and mixing with Officers and Tommies in restaurants and other places. They are spending money and doing themselves well. Refugees cannot do that on the money they were allowed to bring out of Germany. All these Germans have their definite instructions as to what they are to find out . . . .'

Burton was no less vehement in the House of Commons. Information, he intimated, was being given to the enemy by aliens living on the East coast. Their signals to aircraft, if only by means of hanging out their washing, had led to the destruction of British ships on their way to join convoys. To prevent this, he suggested that a thirty-mile area around the coast be designated from which enemy aliens were excluded.

The Home Office was already thinking along similar lines. By the end of March it had made arrangements with local police authorities for all aliens over sixteen in 'protected areas' along the coast to fill in special forms if they wanted to continue to live there. A week later a Home Office order barred residence in these areas to aliens of any nationality after 15 April, unless they had obtained permission from the Home Office or the Chief Constable. The 'protected area' consisted of the areas of Humber, Harwich, Thames, Medway, Dover, Portsmouth, Plymouth, the North of Scotland, Orkney and Shetland and the Firth of Forth.

By the middle of April the situation had changed dramatically. The 'phoney' war had become an all too sobering reality. On 9 April, German troops entered Denmark and moved into Norway, taking Oslo, Bergen, Trondheim and Narvik. Britain was suffering its first reverses. Moreover, it was authoritatively reported that the collapse of Norway had been to a large extent the result of betrayal from within.

'Disquiet about Britain's "Fifth Column" is growing', recorded the *Daily Mail* editorial on 19 April. 'The people ask that doubtful enemy aliens should be immediately interned and all other aliens strictly examined. The traitors of Norway have shown the perils of the enemy within . . . .' 'Is the Home Secretary aware', thundered Colonel Burton on 23 April, 'that on the arrival of the Germans in Norway, they were received by a number of friendly members of the Nazi organisation?' Was he satisfied that 'satisfactory arrangements existed to prevent any such occurrence in this country'? 'Would it not be better', he added, 'to intern the lot and then pick out the good ones?'

Sadly the *Jewish Chronicle* drew the inevitable conclusions. Little doubt remained, it stated on 19 April, that the Regional Advisory Committees would act much more strictly than had the tribunals before them. 'The disclosures regarding the activities of Nazi agents in the Scandinavian countries and Holland have aroused the keenest suspicions. I have good reason to say that any alien who cannot rid himself of even the slightest suspicion of being an enemy of Britain will be interned.' (Four days later Osbert Peake confirmed this prognosis when he stated in the House that 'The onus on every person of German or Austrian nationality is to show cause why he should not be interned, and the policy is to intern any German or Austrian if there is doubt as to his attitude and disposition towards the Allied cause.')

This was the atmosphere in which the Regional Advisory Committees began their work. Ironically, with the storm breaking around their heads, the first reports of their results are surprisingly innocuous. No spies or people prepared to stab Britain in the back were brought to light. On the contrary, the *Jewish Chronicle* correspondent reported that all over the country enemy aliens called to appear before the Committees were telling of the friendly treatment they were receiving.

By 2 May the Home Secretary could state that the Committees had so far heard some 650 cases and recommended the internment of thirty-two people.

But, whatever the views of the fair-minded men (and women) who composed the Committees, there is no gainsaying the fact that in the country as a whole suspicion of the alien was growing. Though the Mass Observation survey at the end of April found no sign that the press campaign for mass internment had fully registered on the masses, there was every sign that the situation was developing, and especially that it was 'becoming the socially done thing to be anti-refugee'.

On 2 May the Joint Intelligence Committee (the senior body of British military and civilian intelligence), reporting on the Norwegian débâcle, placed the presence of 73,000 non-interned enemy aliens high on the list of potential dangers to the safety of the state.

Responding to the atmosphere of the day, Marylebone Borough Council dismissed in the 'interests of public safety' seventeen enemy aliens who had been engaged in ARP (air-raid precaution) work for the previous five months. A Marylebone alderman explained that 'the idea of Germans taking charge of Britons in an air-raid is grotesque, particularly as it is ten chances to one that the man dropping the bomb is his cousin or some relative'.

# 4 May Madness

On 10 May 1940, the world spun into dizzying action. Germany invaded Holland and Belgium. Winston Churchill became Prime Minister of Britain, the feeble Chamberlain government having tottered and fallen during the debate on the Norwegian campaign. The military authorities came to Home Secretary Sir John Anderson, and 'represented that, in view of the imminent risk of invasion it was . . . of the utmost importance that every male alien between 16 and 70 should be removed forthwith from the coastal strip which . . . was the part of the country likely, if invasion took place, to be affected' (so, at least, Sir John told the House of Commons on 22 August).

Anderson did not delay. On Whit Sunday, 12 May, his Home Office order appeared directing the temporary internment of all male Germans and Austrians over sixteen and under sixty (excluding the invalid and infirm) in Hampshire, the Isle of Wight, East and West Sussex, Kent and Essex (excluding the part in the Metropolitan Police District), East and West Suffolk, Norfolk, Cambridgeshire, the Isle of Ely, Huntingdonshire, Rutland, the Soke of Peterborough, Lincolnshire, Yorkshire, Durham, Northumberland, Berwickshire, Roxburghshire, Selkirkshire, Peeblesshire, East and West Lothian, Midlothian, Fife, Kinrossshire, Angus, Kincardineshire, Aberdeenshire, Banffshire, Morayshire, Nairn, Perthshire and Inverness-shire. Male Germans and Austrians were warned not to enter the area without the express permission of the Secretary of State.

Two months after the event Osbert Peake gave some explanation of the government's actions at this time. In the first place, the British public had not been able to realise the difference between the British position in May 1940 and the position of Holland and Belgium. Holland had had a treaty with Germany whereby she could not refuse admission to any German – and some 300,000 had crossed the frontier shortly before the act of aggression. Moreover, both countries were at peace with Germany and were all too anxious to appease her at the time that the disasters took place.

Secondly, when Holland and Belgium had fallen and the military authorities had recommended that the whole of the East and South-East coastal belts be made into a protected area, 'large numbers of aliens were torn up from the shallow roots which they had been able to acquire since they came here and had to remove. They had no jobs, and had to proceed, with public feeling what it was at that time, in the face of suspicion and mistrust. . . . The only practical method of dealing with the situation was, in fact, to intern the males.' It was, said Peake, 'the most humane thing to do'.

A further order on 12 May imposed restrictions on all other male aliens in the same age-group, regardless of their nationality. They had to report daily to the police-station in person. They could not use any motor-vehicle (except public transport) or bicycle. And they had to observe a curfew between eight in the evening and six in the morning. Chief Constables were, however, authorised to grant exemptions in certain cases if they were satisfied they would not prejudice the national interest.

The Home Office 'recognised and much regretted that these necessary measures will involve for a period great hardship in individual cases. Those persons, however, who are affected by them and who are in fact, faithful to the vital interests of this country will give the best proof of their attitude by submitting freely and uncomplainingly to the restrictions which the exigencies of the situation for the moment require.'

By Sunday evening, 3000 Germans and Austrians, whatever their tribunal rating, who fortuitously found themselves in the affected area had been interned. They were taken entirely without warning by local police and conveyed to military centres before finding more permanent refuge in internment camps.

Who was actually in the coastal area at the fateful moment when the police swooped was already a matter of chance. Several undergraduates at Cambridge University fell within the net – some only two weeks before the Tripos examinations. It is heartening to note that they were none the less approved for admission to their BA degrees without further examination. Pastor Ehrhardt's presence in the protected area was also fortuitous. 'My husband would never have been interned at all if we had not happened to be in Sussex at the time. We were category "C"', writes Mrs E. R. Ehrhardt. 'As it was, the police were waiting when a German clergyman, who shared the house, and my husband, who was not yet ordained, returned on Sunday afternoon from preaching on the Methodist circuit. The minister, having recruited them as his lay preachers, had been called up.'

After being deprived of his position as lecturer in Roman and civil law in Frankfurt because of his teachings, Arnold Ehrhardt read theology at Basel. He completed his studies and came to England in July 1939. His widow writes, 'I took the children to England in February 1939. When Hitler marched into Prague [in March 1939] a teacher said to me a war might be very unpleasant for us. I answered we were in England precisely because we preferred an English camp to the German ones . . . .

'In Sussex, the men were first taken to Seaford – state secret, the whole village talked about it, though I learnt it rather later than most.'

The internment Order caused as many anomalies by its selection of areas as it did by the timing of its enforcement. Martin Ostwald in Bournemouth (Hampshire) was interned. His brother in neighbouring Poole (Dorset) was left at large. Aged sixteen and fifteen respectively, they had come to England on a children's transport in March 1939, hoping eventually to be reunited with their parents in America. They had been imprisoned in the concentration camp at Sachsenhausen after *Kristallnacht*, and then stayed for a short period in Holland.

Martin Ostwald told me, 'On 12 May 1940 I was interned. I was working at a hotel when the police came for me. They were very nice and said they had to take me away for a short time. I was to pack my things as I might have to stay overnight. I was relieved – this will shock you – but my parents were still in Germany; I had been corresponding with them and therefore the Germans knew my address. I had heard that German parachutists had paved the way for the invasion of the Low Countries, and I was deadly afraid that the Germans would parachute down one night and tell me at pistol-point to take them to the nearest airport on pain of harming my parents. So I was relieved to be in protective custody.

'We were almost immediately taken to buses and then driven to Southampton. There we were put into a huge gymnasium. There were palliasses put on the floor, and there we slept. There were all sorts of people: Jews and non-Jews. One man, I remember, spoke no German at all: he had come over after the First World War; he was not Jewish. We were there certainly not for more than a week. Then we were taken by train to Huyton [Lancashire].'

Ulrich Skaller was also taken to Huyton at that time. He had been in England for his family timber business in November 1938 when he had received a telegram from his wife in Poland: 'Don't come back. Get permission to stay in England and bring us over.' For a while he carried on a timber business in England, but wartime regulations put paid to this. The week after 10 May 1940 was to be the first time the small rubber-factory he then opened would produce something saleable and make some money.

Skaller told me, 'On Sunday 12 May I was in the morning in Leigh-on-Sea. My uncle and all my family were in category "C". We could travel freely, though I think we had to give our cameras to the police. There were some little restrictions but nothing serious. Anyway that day I went to see my uncle to go into a little wood to see bluebells with a Christian friend of ours. Two plain-clothes policemen appeared and interned my uncle and his twin sons, who were twenty. Another policeman went home with me. He said, "You must take your shaving kit, food for twenty-four hours, and one or two changes of clothing. Pack and come with me." When my wife started to cry, the policeman embraced her and said, "Don't cry. Your husband will be well treated. It will only be a few days before we sort out the good from the bad."

'At Southend police-station the Chief Constable addressed us. We were two coach-loads, about sixty people, I guess. He said, "I have to intern you but please feel that no stigma is attached to you through this. But after what has happened in Holland we must take this precaution. And a lot of innocent ones have to suffer with the few black sheep." And then we boarded the two coaches, destination unknown.

'It turned out to be Warley Barracks, Brentwood, and there came also a lot of internees from all over Essex. We were in the gymnasium of the barracks, a big exercise hall. We were bedded on the floor with palliasses. There we remained for ten or fourteen days under guard. We were not allowed to communicate with our families. This was for all of us a very great weight on our minds and also for our families. The treatment, and especially the food, at Warley was excellent. We got full military rations in the military dining-hall: a hot cooked breakfast, a good lunch (the main meal) and then a light meal in the evening – and plenty of tea. There was always at meals an officer present who went from table to table and asked, "Any complaints?" And I remember that there was special food for diabetics provided or for other medical cases. And I think also kosher food for orthodox people. There was a rabbi amongst us. We had Friday evening prayers and I think daily prayers, for those who wanted them. We had also several doctors amongst us who were asked to treat anybody in need of medical help and were in contact with the regimental doctors for medicine and so on.

'After about ten days, we were divided into two parties. The first party was sent away, destination unknown. But the military were anxious that families would not be parted. My uncle's sons were at first to go with the first party, but at his request they were left. Two or three days later, the rest of us lined up in the yard. The military escort were charging their rifles in front of us. We were marched to Brentwood station, where we boarded a train. We were in a third-class carriage, but it was a decent train; destination unknown – but we looked out of the windows at the stations. First it went north, then west. Somebody had already heard something about a camp at Huyton and the rumour went round. It proved to be right.'

Eugen Glueckauf followed a similar trail, though he missed out the Huyton experience. He had left Germany in April 1933 after obtaining his doctorate and working as a research student at the Technical University of Berlin. At the outbreak of war he was working at the University of Durham. He told me, 'Shortly after my arrival at Durham, the Meteorological Office cancelled my contract on account of the war. However, the University went on employing me, and we moved to the University Observatory, where I did the daily weather records in addition to my research. This was greatly frowned on by security. But nothing happened until the invasion of Holland, except that we had to register and our radio was taken away. I also went before a tribunal and was classified "C".

'On Whit Sunday 1940 the police called at our house: it was only to be an interrogation for a day or so.

'I was taken to Fenham Barracks, Newcastle, where I found a multitude of similarly inconvenienced people. No one could give you any information. We couldn't communicate with anybody. We could have one visit from a member of the family to get some necessities for a long stay. Irma came and brought me some shirts and pyjamas. I spent three "pleasant" days in Fenham. The food was army rations and very good. For breakfast we had bacon, three eggs and tomatoes. What was not so good was the latrine, because the barracks were intended for a few hundred people and they now held thousands. This caused great difficulties and long queues. But most people realised that other refugees taken over by the Germans in Holland were worse off.'

# 5 The Paltriest Kitchen Maid

The press approved these measures. But they were not enough. 'There will be security only when all of them are safely under guard', proclaimed the *Evening News* on 13 May, the day General Rommel's 7th Panzer Division crossed the Meuse near Dinant and Guderian crossed the Meuse near Sedan, marking the German entry into France.

The next day, a memorandum on the 'Fifth Column Menace', written by the British minister at the Hague, Sir Neville Bland, was circulated in Whitehall. It echoed this view. 'The paltriest kitchen maid, with German connections', it warned, 'not only can be but generally is, a menace to the safety of the country. . . . I have not the least doubt that, when the signal is given . . . there will be satellites of the monster all over the country who will at once embark on widespread sabotage and attacks on civilians and the military indiscriminately. We cannot afford to take the risk. *All* Germans and Austrians at least ought to be interned at once.'

A Mass Observation report at that juncture suggests that Bland was preaching to the converted. 'The Dutch parachute news, and the news of their linking up with aliens already in Holland, had a deeper, immediate and "alarming" effect. Now the enemy in our midst is easily visualised. The always latent antagonism to the alien and foreigner began to flare up. Nearly everyone, as previous research has shown, is latently somewhat anti-semitic and somewhat anti-alien. But ordinarily it is not the done thing to express such sentiments publicly. The news from Holland made it quite the done thing all of a sudden . . . .'

On 15 May, fighting in Holland ceased.

On 16 May, the Joint Intelligence Committee urgently recommended – and its recommendation was endorsed by the Chiefs of Staff – that internment be extended to all enemy aliens, male and female, between the ages of sixteen and seventy. The same day, the Home Office took limited action on this advice: all category 'B' male aliens between the ages of sixteen and sixty were interned.

*The Times* of 17 May reported, 'Immediately after the issue of the Home Office Order a round-up of enemy aliens in the Metropolitan area began. Members of Scotland Yard's Criminal Investigation Department at once acted on information gathered while they were inquiring into the credentials of enemy aliens in the first instance. The whole of Scotland Yard's fleet of motor-cars from headquarters and police-stations in divisions were mobilised, and Chief Officers were on duty throughout Wednesday night. . . . The greatest secrecy was maintained by Scotland Yard and even the Officers concerned had no idea of what was afoot until they were given instructions when reporting for duty yesterday morning. . . .

'At Sheffield two motor-coach loads were rounded up and they were accompanied by two lorries manned by soldiers. Many of the aliens detained in Glasgow were businessmen. A number of them carried well packed suitcases when they arrived at the police headquarters. . . . In all cases they accepted the position quietly, the majority having apparently been expecting the new order.'

'The step was obviously unavoidable in the presence of the mounting danger of the preparatory German undermining of countries destined for Nazi attack', wrote the editor of the *Jewish Chronicle*. 'As such, it has been cheerfully accepted by the genuine refugees concerned, helped by the consideration shown by the British authorities – a humanity in glaring contrast with the brutal methods of the jackbooted Prussian.'

The aliens, it would appear from an anecdote in the *Chronicle*, were giving proof of patriotism as well as cheerful acceptance. Many of those rounded up in London were first taken to the barracks at Albany Street under close guard. A military band was playing in the courtyard. When it struck up 'God Save the King' the refugees rose as a man and stood to attention. When it was ended, they clapped enthusiastically. The guards, the *Chronicle* tells us, smiled.

Heinz Edgar Kiewe, emigrant, was amongst those in this wave of internments. He had come to London from Königsberg in March 1933 and had become London editor of the *Konfektioner*, a textile journal. Kiewe told me, 'We were living in Ealing and in Ealing in 1939 a refugee hostel was founded. My niece and I volunteered to give our social help on Saturdays and Sundays and that is how the first chapter of the Popular University began. I invited the refugees of Ealing to give lectures in German and I was surprised how pleased they were that they were acknowledged in England.

'One morning in May 1940 I was arrested at six o'clock and taken to Knightsbridge Grenadier Barracks. My mother had already packed my trunk. My mother and father were both interned, although my father was already sixty-two.

'We were about thirty people in one room at Knightsbridge and the majority were completely distressed: they considered that their lives were ruined. But we had amongst us in our company a man called Bilbo who told us that he had been the guard of the gangster Al Capone, that he had become a captain of Spanish revolutionaries, and heaps of other sensational things. Bilbo was the son of a Berlin Jewish family. His grandparents and parents had been millionaires. Although he had an English mother he was international and of enormous physical size. He was an anarchist and called everyone, academic and non-academic, by bad names; he thus levelled internees down to internees. He had a great sense of humour, and once said, "Boys, when we come out of this barrack and are shipped to the Isle of Man, I will arrange the *Beggar's Opera!*" This was the first sign to me of the joy of being interned: to come into an adventurous and spiritually new sphere.'

Inexplicably, also taken at the same time as the category 'B' men were those who had not as yet been through a tribunal. One such was Peter Katz. He had come to Britain in 1934 with his family. Katz told me, 'I had a German passport issued in 1933 and valid for five years, then I became stateless. But, in any case, any foreigner living here was issued with an aliens' registration book. The tribunals in 1939–40 applied to all aliens between sixteen and sixty-five. I wasn't sixteen at that stage and that was the cause of my internment. I wasn't classified. I was a child. Everyone else in our family was "C". I was still at the crammers preparing for Matric[ulation] in summer 1940.

'The invasion of the Low Countries in May 1940 really was the beginning of my internment. In March I was sixteen. By that time the tribunals had already classified everybody and they used to sit two or three times a year to classify bods like me. But there hadn't been one between March and May 1940. I think my mother got a greater shock than I did because two plain-clothes men came to the door when I was away and wanted to talk to me. That was done in a very underhand way because we were told, "Just pack a toothbrush. You'll only be away a few days."

'That evening saw me at Hendon police-station, where I was joined by two other people: one of them was a boy like myself, sixteen and unclassified. But the other! We had little attaché cases with a change of underwear and a shirt. But the third man, who was in his twenties, had brought a whacking great suitcase. In my know-all way, I smiled at him and said, was he moving house? He said, "I've been through this before . . . ." He was classified "A" but had been released and then retaken on 16 May.

'From Hendon I was taken to Chelsea Barracks, a Guards' barracks. It was the only time I've been in a Black Maria so far. The barracks were crowded. They put palliasses down side by side and there was hardly room to turn over. I was not terrified but worried. At this place we met the father of the other boy from Hendon. He was a very able man, very resolute; he took me in tow.'

Moses Aberbach was another unclassified. He came to England from Vienna on a children's transport on 12 December 1938. Aberbach told me, 'On 16 May 1940, a month after my sixteenth birthday, I was interned. It was a beautiful spring day. I had just returned home from morning service at a Leeds synagogue. A detective, a young man, well-mannered and impeccably dressed, came to our house and said I'd have to come with him. We took a tram to town and he even made me pay my own fare. We were taken first of all to the city gaol, my only acquaintance with the inside of a gaol. There were some regular gaolbirds there who looked at us in astonishment and tried to communicate. They were all excited when we arrived and began shouting in their (to us incomprehensible) gaol dialect. We were, however, segregated from them, and found ourselves in a very large cell with standing-room only for most of us. Sanitation was somewhat primitive and, apart from tap-water, we had nothing to eat or drink until the late afternoon, when we were given a tasteless cheese sandwich. I was classified as German because I was born in Vienna and Vienna was in Austria and Austria had been occupied by Germany. My parents, on the other hand, had been born in Galicia and were therefore Polish. According to both Austrian and Polish law, children under age shared the citizenship of their parents.

'We were then taken out and conveyed by buses to an army barracks in Pontefract near Leeds. A few days later my parents were able to visit me, bring me some goodies and reassure themselves, God forbid, that I was not in a concentration camp. It was not, to be sure, the most comfortable place on earth. We stayed there for about two weeks. Pontefract was a huge barracks where the walls were lined with mattresses. There were tables in the middle where we, some 200 of us, ate, and washrooms at the other end. We learned to manage with cold showers which did not entirely wash away the dust accumulated through sitting all day on mattresses placed on a dusty floor. There was no kosher food. I didn't eat the soup or the meat, but there was enough without them. We were given army rations. I had brought all my books for the School Certificate exams with me; in fact, I was loaded with books. Practically everyone else had brought books too. We were most of us Jewish refugees. There were a few real Germans and also a couple of Nazis, one of whom was a brilliant lecturer; I heard him lecture on Shakespeare. There were also Communists from the Sudetenland. These Communists threatened to beat up the Nazis, so the Nazis kept quiet after that. We had daily religious services and an hour's exercise outside every day, when we were surrounded by soldiers. No one ill-treated us. Our only complaint was that we were interned at all.'

# 6 Escape to Freedom

It was not only from the British Isles that enemy aliens were being swept into internment camps. Some, washed up on the beaches, suffered similar fate. After desperate and successful attempts to escape the Nazi invaders, some German Jews eventually reached safety and freedom in democratic Britain.

Kurt and Freda, and Marie and Otto Neurath were among some fifty people who escaped from the beach at Scheveringen, Holland, on 14 May, the day the Netherlands surrendered. They found places in the official lifeboat of South Holland, manned on that occasion by students from the technical high school at Delft. They were picked up by a British destroyer. Kurt told me, 'They landed us at darkened Dover and separated us. I protested but they said, "You will see one another tomorrow." Tomorrow came several weeks later. I was taken to Dover police-station with all the men from our boat – about twenty of us. Many people went hysterical; some had poison on them. We were taken to Pentonville prison in London. There, we had our first synagogue service in England; there was a big synagogue there. The rabbi told us how far the German armies had got in France. We protested violently the whole time; we didn't want to be in prison. They took us to the worst part; we had to clean it all up. They stripped us naked and our hair was searched to see if we were carrying secret messages. After two days, during which we only had half-an-hour's exercise in the prison yard for shaving or fresh air, they opened the cell-doors during the day on condition that we wouldn't overstep the threshold. We then had the opportunity to meet other people and to tell our stories.'

Freda said, 'It was much worse for me because I was expecting this baby and I was nearly five months pregnant when we arrived. We were taken to Holloway prison but I had no idea that I was in prison. I didn't believe it for two days. I wouldn't believe that they could take me to prison. It was absolutely traumatic. I was a child, twenty years old, and very spoilt. I didn't know anything. I had never been away from my family before. I just couldn't believe it. We were searched, bathed and put into cells. My cell-door said ENEMY ALIEN – on my cell-door! It was incredible. I didn't tell anyone I was expecting, but Kurt had told a friend and she told the Holloway people. I fought them like a hyena when they tried to examine me. I was so agitated they gave me bromide. I thought it was something to do away with the baby. I slapped the bromide away, screaming, "I want my baby!" They took me to the hospital wing. We were locked up for twenty-three and a half hours a day, and only allowed out for half an hour. I had to wash all my clothes every night and hang them round my cell to dry. We fetched the water from a central point for this. There was a woman there with a terribly high-pitched voice; every time I heard it I fainted.

'When they found I was too hysterical, they sent me back to the rest of our group. I had a craving for an apple and I just couldn't get one. I saw some in another cell when I went out for exercise. I could have stolen one but I didn't. All we got to eat was slop: bits of meat in water – and bread. It was dreadful. I was there for three weeks. I couldn't lie on my pillow any more; it was stuffed with straw. I used to stand by the bars of my cell and when anyone went by I used to shout: "I done nothing! I done nothing!" In the half-hour we were allowed out, we mixed with other prisoners. We used to ask them, "What did you do?" and they would answer things like "I poisoned my husband".'

Marie Neurath met Kurt and Freda on board the Dutch lifeboat. Marie told me, 'At Dover our passports had to be shown and we were sorted out. Otto and I were asked to enter a little booth and Otto was taken away. I was suddenly alone in the world. Then I was called into the booth again and there was this couple, Kurt and Freda. I thought they needed an interpreter. I suddenly had someone to look after. Then we were joined by two other women with little girls; they were separated from their brother.

'We were taken by train to Victoria and put in a room with some officials. They didn't know what to do with us. I heard them talking about me: "She's an able-bodied woman." We were put in a coach and taken to Fulham Institute. It was a Dickensian poor-house and we had blankets on the floor. There was a woman walking with high heels, clack, clack, clack. I didn't sleep that night. Our first meal in Dover had been corned beef with sharp English mustard and boiled potatoes. It was difficult to swallow but we were very hungry. We German women were kept together with the Dutch. We were given a very hot bath and investigated medically. I asked, "Can I use the telephone?" and I rang a friend and asked her to come and see me. She came straight away. I wrote to Susan Stebbings, a friend of Otto's, to tell her we were in England and I asked if I could give the letter to my friend to post. "Yes." So people now knew about our position. We were only there one night and then there came a big lorry. I had asked the customs officer for Otto's address: Pentonville prison, and all the time I was hoping that they'd take us there too.

'We were taken to Holloway. At first we were put in little boxes like chicken-boxes. We were allowed to use the toilet but had to keep the door open. Then we were stripped and investigated and given another bath and also a toothbrush and a nightshirt. Then we were asked what our religion was and were given the appropriate form of Bible. It was nice to have a book to read. Then we were taken to our cells – we each had separate cells. I stupidly said that Freda was expecting a baby and she was taken to hospital. She was so unhappy there that she was brought back. It was wonderful to have a single cell: we could sleep and sleep and sleep (after two sleepless nights). We were even allowed to lie down in the daytime.

'We were three weeks in prison. We got enough to eat and were never hungry there. We had exercise in the prison-court, where there was grass, and we were told to move about and not just sit. We walked and talked with each other. Later, they allowed us to leave our doors open and visit each other. We got busy: everyone had a little blackboard and a piece of chalk. Some started Spanish lessons. I drew Otto on my blackboard and my brother on the other side, so sometimes I had one, sometimes the other. We were given books and wool. We had to knit stockings for soldiers: it was a pleasure. We were given a cloth to clean our cell and I also cleaned my windows. No one else had thought of this; they came into my cell and said, "Why does yours look better?" I liked to look out of my windows at the hills.

'We heard from the other wing the Horstwessel song, so we knew there were Nazi people there. We met them at church services; we were allowed to go and I went for the change. There was a chaplain who came from cell to cell. I said to this chaplain, "Thank you very much. I don't need comfort. I am not a criminal with a bad conscience." When we were put in prison our handbags were taken away; one could ask for a comb back.

'I had my birthday in Holloway and said, "Now you must change my age on my card." I got a few daisies someone had picked in the yard. Then Rosy Hahn also had her birthday and I made up a little poem. I got some toilet paper and made copies and distributed them, so that we had a small choir. Rosy sang Schubert to us and tears ran down our cheeks.

'I can only remember the Dutch verse of the birthday song. It went as follows:

> Wij zijn in geen hemel,
> Wij zijn in geen hel;
> Wij zijn niet in Alkmaar,
> Wij zijn in de cel.

which translated means,

> We are in no heaven,
> We are in no hell;
> We are not in Alkmaar,
> We are in the cell.

Rosy had lived as a refugee in Alkmaar, Holland.'

# 7 First Stop: Kempton Park

After only seven days in Pentonville and while Freda was languishing in Holloway, Kurt was taken to Kempton Park racecourse. Large numbers of internees passed through the transit camp which was established there.

Leon Feldman remembers the 'arrival of a whole lot of refugees from Holland. We had very little news: the stories they told us! There was a former judge and a big fat guy who was a banker, and many others who had paid with gold to save their lives. And Britain interned them!'

It was very much an Army camp. 'The Grenadier Guards were in charge of us', Peter Katz, who was taken there on 17 May, told me, 'and they treated us like prisoners of war; they marched around with pistols in their hands and shouted orders. There were two roll-calls a day outside. It was a hot summer.' Leon Feldman remembers 'a scary feeling being there because the soldiers all carried mounted bayonets. Some of them were very sympathetic and some were very harsh, to which we were not used. It showed that they had not been told whom they were guarding. The first evening there was a general assembly, an *appel*. The brigadier was a big, tall fellow. He had been called back from France, where he had been a field-officer. He admitted that he was disappointed. He thought he would be guarding prisoners of war and they gave him the job of guarding rabbits!'

The attitude of the military did have its funny side. Peter Katz tells how 'After about ten days a Black Maria drew up outside and out stepped two Grenadier Guards with rifles. Next came a little boy in short trousers, and then another two Grenadier Guards. It was the boy's sixteenth birthday either that day or the next. He lived in Hampstead Garden suburb. The camp was surrounded with barbed wire and there were guards all round. That was a good camp: we were all ages and all social types; what is more it was not overcrowded. The food was tolerable there and it was served by the army; we used to queue up for it canteen fashion. We slept on palliasses.

'There I was very lucky. They were using all parts of the building. We were in the King's enclosure with His toilet at one end and Her toilet at the other. They were very luxurious toilets, with marble slabs. Everyone envied us.'

Leon Feldman was assigned to the stables: 'All sorts of cultural activities started immediately. There were lectures and music and some people were preparing for Matric.'

Heinz Kiewe is more specific: 'From the first morning, Bilbo mounted the bandstand and shrieked, "Cabaret! Cabaret! Cabaret!" With his cheerful shrieky voice, all people came. They had nothing else to do. "Any of you who can demonstrate anything, come up here!" So we had a strong man, a gymnast, a magician, singers, musicians – Peter Stadlen and a little chap of seventeen who was later with the Amadeus String Quartet – and everyone had a good time. We did it the second day again, but the attraction was already vanishing and I discussed with Bilbo about giving a talk. I had lectured at Kitchener camp about the problems of foreigners in England and called it "Britain and its Bloody Foreigners". I gave this talk on the bandstand on the third day and three officers observed the lecture but did not interfere.

'Most of the refugees had only come recently, and hearing about my many years living in England seemed to have more confidence and asked where could one learn English. I discussed the matter with Bilbo and suggested the Popular University. Lecturers immediately applied, being delighted to express themselves. The best English-speaking refugee in the camp was my friend Theo Marx. He was only eighteen but had been at Mill Hill School.'

Not everything was perfect, however. Peter Katz expresses a major source of worry: 'What was bad was that we were out of touch completely with our relatives and friends. I don't think that we were allowed to write from there.'

Kurt had a financial problem: 'They had searched our pockets in Pentonville and put a list of all our belongings in the prison book. They took everything away and then gave it back after seven days. I had in my pocket 75 Dutch guilders and I could not prove that I had had them at Kempton Park. A lieutenant made me deny at pistol-point that I had had them. When I was at Kempton Park, I was the book-keeper at the camp bank.'

What caused distress to many internees was the company they found themselves among. Peter Katz might have enjoyed mixing with 'all social types'; Feldman and Kiewe, perhaps because they were slightly older, did not. 'As soon as we got there', Feldman says, 'there was a big to-do because of the people they had there. Non-Jewish refugees we would not have objected to, but we saw all these people there – Italians they had picked up in Soho! Communists! Germans! I met the great-grandson of the Kaiser there, Prince Frederick. He looked like Prince Philip, a long thin, fair face. They all look the same, these people. We were interviewed and had to give our addresses, and he gave his as "care of Queen Mary, Buckingham Palace".

'We formed ourselves into a Jewish group. We felt that because of our deep Jewish commitment, we shouldn't be thrown in with all these others. We understood that Britain had to protect herself against the Communists and revolution, and of course against the Nazis – but not against us. Our record spoke for itself. There were also our dietary needs: we didn't want to eat non-kosher food.'

'The very orthodox Jews I remember in particular', Heinz Kiewe told me. 'But we did find very strange people in the camp. About 60 per cent were Jews and 20 per cent were Germans who had lived for twenty to twenty-five years in England. We had seven rabbis.

'We also had Protestants, Catholics, Sudeten Germans who because they said they were not Czechs but Germans were interned. They did the laundry of the camp and also baked the most beautiful bread and cakes. On the second day, we discovered that there was in the camp the master spy of the First World War, Captain Franz von Rintelen. He told us that he had been invited to England by a British admiral because he said he was anti-Hitler. He also said that he had seen Mr Chamberlain. Also interned was the legal adviser of von Ribbentrop. He left the camp every morning for the commandant's office; we had this information from our British comrades on the other side of the wire. (They said, "Why aren't we inside? You have such a good time!")

'Anyway, we asked the commandant for a meeting and expressed our horror that we were interned with such dangerous people. I threatened that, if this legal adviser were not removed instantly, I would report it to our friends in the House of Commons. I told him that we knew who the Nazis were; we had better eyes for Nazis than they did. I was warned that if I tried to make difficulties I would be moved to a mental hospital. Two days later, Nazi ambassador

Ribbentrop's legal adviser was moved to another camp, where his cousin was.

'At one stage he was asked to go to the commandant to help him make a list of members of the Communist Party amongst the refugees.'

Some light might perhaps have been shed on Kurt's lost guilders by a court-case which took place a year later. A certain Major James Braybrook, an officer in the Corps of Military Police, was charged with stealing 100 gold sovereigns, two typewriters, various large sums in foreign currency, 1000 safety razor blades, and a number of sixpenny novels.

The Major had been commissioned at the outbreak of war and became adjutant and quartermaster of a camp for internees. In May 1940 he was appointed commandant of a similar camp elsewhere, and later was dispatched to be commandant of another camp, which had 1000 internees.

The 100 gold sovereigns, said prosecuting counsel, were the property of a German who took them with him to Pentonville gaol, where they were entered in the prison property book. The sovereigns were placed in a white linen bag and subsequently taken with the owner to the internment-camp, where Major Braybrook was commandant. At the camp, counsel said, all the internees' belongings were thrown into a waste-paper basket by the Major, no attempt being made to identify specific articles. When the escorting officer asked for a receipt for the valuables, he replied, 'They will get that if they are lucky!'

In July 1941 Braybrook was sentenced at the Central Criminal Court to eighteen months imprisonment.

'Our few silver guilders', Kurt concludes the episode, 'were later refunded by the British authorities and exchanged by the Dutch.'

# 8 Women and Children First

The ten days following the internment of 'B' category men saw the rapid deterioration of the military situation. German forces swept through Belgium and advanced rapidly into France. On 27 May Belgium surrendered. The same day, the evacuation of the British Expeditionary Force, trapped in the small French port of Dunkirk by encircling German units, began. In Britain it seemed that the anticipated German invasion could only be weeks away.

On 18 May, Winston Churchill made his first speech as Prime Minister in the House of Commons: 'I would say to the House, as I have said to those who have joined this Government: I have nothing to offer but blood, toil, tears and sweat.'

And in his first broadcast, on 24 May: 'One bond unites us all, to wage war until victory is won and never to surrender ourselves to servitude and shame, whatever the cost and the agony may be. . . . Upon all . . . the long night of barbarism will descend . . . unless we conquer, as conquer we must, as conquer we shall.'

Pressure for the internment of all enemy aliens in the country mounted as fears of direct enemy attack increased. 'Act! Act! Act!' screamed the *Daily Mail* on 24 May. 'The round-up of enemy aliens must be taken out of the fumbling hands of the local tribunals. All refugees from Austria, Germany and Czechoslovakia, men and women alike, should be drafted without delay to a remote part of the country and kept under strict supervision.'

In the House of Lords, the mood was similar if more restrained. The Duke of Devonshire, Under Secretary of State for India, was one of the few to plead the cause of moderation. 'To intern the whole of these category "C" aliens', he argued, 'would not only be unjust and cruel, but also it would be a gross waste of effort and manpower which we can ill afford in this grave emergency.'

Sir John Anderson in the Cabinet was also advocating moderation. In a report on 17 May he predicted that, 'If thousands of women, including pregnant women and young children, were subjected to the conditions of barrack-room life in some sort of internment-camp, there would soon be a public outcry against this treatment.' And at a Cabinet meeting on 24 May he backed this up by pointing out 'that the military authorities should recognise that arrangements made for prisoner-of-war camps were totally unsuitable for detaining internees and suspects. Very special precautions were necessary for the latter.'

On 22 May Anderson had in fact acted – but in a somewhat different direction, and one long urged by refugee and other bodies. At the beginning of April the *Jewish Chronicle* had already warned of three dangers which could result from general internment. First, it would place an additional burden on the state; secondly, potentially valuable labour would be forced into expensive idleness; lastly, it would lead 'the treason-hunters sadly off the trail', since it would give the impression that the work of treacherously helping the enemy could be undertaken only by alien residents.

On 25 April Anderson showed that he was alive to this last danger when he told the House of Commons that he had 'for some time been carefully watching the activities of certain small groups of people, of whom some appear to be deliberately anxious to hinder the war effort'. When the question had been debated, however, it had been generally agreed 'that every effort should be made, even in time of war, to avoid interference with the propagation of opinions held by small minorities'.

When on the following day J. G. Braithwaite (MP for Holderness in the East Riding of Yorkshire) asked in the House for the internment of Sir Oswald Mosley, leader of the British Union of Fascists (BUF), he was told by Osbert Peake that 'There is no evidence in my possession to show that Sir Oswald Mosley is a member of a Nazi organisation.'

In the climate of 22 May, a paragraph was added to Defence Regulation 18b by Order in Council, giving the Home Secretary powers to intern persons of British nationality whom he had good reason to believe were members of an organisation in sympathy with the enemy. That same night, Sir Oswald and thirty-five other leading members of the BUF were arrested. They were joined a week later by 346 of their followers. The BUF was dissolved and its publications banned.

But, important as this step was, it did not distract attention from the alien menace. On 27 May Sir John acted again. A letter was sent to Chief Constables all over the country instructing them to prepare to arrest all German and Austrian category 'B' women between the ages of sixteen and sixty. Only the invalid and infirm and those in an advanced state of pregnancy were to be excluded. Mothers could take any children under the age of sixteen with them – again, if a child were dangerously ill, the mother was exempt.

Arrests, the letter instructed, should be carried out as a general rule in the early morning and the police were to enlist feminine assistance in the performance of this delicate task: a police woman, a police matron, perhaps a member of the Women's Voluntary Service. The arrested women should be allowed to take one suitcase each and anything else they could carry, such as a rug. In fact, they were to be advised to take as much warm clothing as possible. 'Women should be given reasonable time to pack their requirements for the journey', the letter stated. 'They should be informed that it might be two or more days before they reach their destination.'

The police were also ordered to search the houses of these women and inform MI5 of 'any information suggesting the existence of plans for assisting the enemy'.

All in all, some 3500 women were interned as a result of this measure, 1500 of them from the London area. 'In some instances in London', *The Times* reported on 28 May, 'the police had to wait at houses until the women had dressed. By noon several hundreds had been taken to special centres. The great majority seemed to be under thirty, and most of them appeared to be of the domestic-servant class. Each carried a small, tightly packed suitcase, and some also had paper parcels. Many mothers took their children with them.

'At one of the London receiving centres there were young nuns, babies only a few weeks old, and boys and girls. One group of young women were fashionably dressed, and each had a fur coat. Several of the older women were in tears. All carried gas masks.'

The government's action in interning these women brought sharply into the limelight the first problem the *Chronicle* had predicted in April. Some 10 per cent of the women, it was estimated, were supporting families. Without their earnings to rely on, their families became a charge upon the state and the refugee organisations.

Each wave of internment had called forth its own story of the distress of those left at home. 'I myself was outside,' writes Mrs Ehrhardt, 'which meant trying to send comforts with money we had not got and dealing with my four children in a London hostel, five for much of the time, as I had been handed a small girl, both of whose parents were interned.'

'A few days after I had been taken away for internment', said Eugen Glueckauf, 'Irma had got notice from the police to leave Durham; it was too near the coast. She had to go to Leeds. There was no one to look after her; and she went into a Quaker hostel. My mother was there too. Irma didn't get on with her and decided to leave. She found two ladies who took her in. She was fully occupied with our baby. Irma was not quite without resources: she had her savings (about £100) which she had transferred from Germany before leaving. She had no income during that time.'

In the atmosphere of the day, these arguments fell on deaf ears. The internment of 'B' grade women was a reality. Edith Jacobus was amongst their number. She had come to London with her husband and child in August 1936, leaving Berlin, where they had owned a glue-factory.

'We made a living until 1939, when the war broke out and we were given "B". Later, the order came for my husband to pack a few things, hardly anything, just one suit. He was sent to Onchan on the Isle of Man. It took six weeks till I got the first news where he was.

'I was in London letting rooms and getting money from Bloomsbury House. By and by I sold everything valuable in the house: Bohemian glasses, camera, typewriter, diamonds – anything to make a living. And I was worried stiff.

'Then came the day when all the women of interned men were collected, even women of sixty. Overnight came the law. There was a knock at the door: "Will you please get ready. You will be taken for security reasons to the Isle of Man."'

Dr H. had worked as a doctor in a hospital in Vienna. After a period in Denmark, she came to England in 1938 on a domestic permit. She was not allowed to practice her profession but did eventually obtain a nursing permit and a position with a private family.

'I was interned the same day as Dunkirk. The husband of my patient was a JP. Some days before, a gentleman came and asked me, "Are you worried to be here?" Lincolnshire at that time was a protected area. I said, "Of course not", and "I can't leave my patient in these anxious times." Two days later two policemen came and told me to pack a small suitcase for the weekend, only for some interrogations. I only had my toilet-case and a couple of books, strangely enough, about Wagner. I was taken to the police-station and eventually to a boat.'

Yet, when Sir John Anderson informed the House of Commons on 30 May that he had interned all 'Bs' between sixteen and sixty, it was still not enough for some members. 'Is the Minister aware', asked Vice-Admiral Taylor (MP for South Paddington), that the age limit of sixty does not automatically prohibit anybody above that age from doing harm to this country if he wishes to do so?' 'Is [it] not the Minister's opinion that a man over sixty might be a danger to England, seeing what a great danger to Germany is the Prime Minister, who is sixty-five?' asked Seymour Cocks (MP for Broxtowe, Nottingham).

By this time, 5600 men and 3200 women had been interned.

# 9 Luxurious Idleness

In May 1940 proprietors of hotels and boarding-houses at Port Erin, Edwardian seaside resort on the south-west corner of the Isle of Man, were asked by a representative of the Home Office if they would be prepared to accommodate internees in return for payment of three shillings per person per day. Prospects for the season in that summer of 1940 did not seem rosy. Most of them were happy to agree.

Dame Joanna Cruickshank was appointed commandant of Rushen camp established there. From the beginning, the administration of the women's internment-camps was the responsibility of the Home Office.

Many of the 'B' category women arrested on 27 May were brought directly here with their children, after only a few days in transit.

'When we arrived on the Isle of Man, the inhabitants stood watching us refugees arrive and do you know what they did? They spat on us as nasty Germans', said Edith Jacobus. 'We were taken by train and bus together with real Nazis to Port Erin. Amongst us were non-Jewish maids and things who were employed in Britain.'

'I can remember on the train in the Isle of Man', says Dr H. 'I wanted to cheer the other girls up. I made them sing. They were mostly domestics in my compartment'.

They were joined very shortly by the 'Dutch' contingent from Holloway. Freda relates, 'In our place [Holloway] everything happened at night. And they always answered our questions, all of them, "I don't know; there's a war on." "Where are we going?" "Where's my husband?" "I don't know; there's a war on." Anyway, one night we were woken and taken to Liverpool and to a sailors' hostel there. The journey was at night. We asked the policemen who were escorting us where we were going. "I don't know; there's a war on." My craving for apples got greater and greater and greater. I nearly went out of my mind.

'Two nights later we were taken to the docks and went to the Isle of Man – but again we were not told. A few people were left behind in the cells and this was a mistake. They were later bombarded and a very nice old lady lost her mind. That day, when we went across the water by boat, was the first time I was ready to take my life. I stood at the end of the boat and felt that it just wasn't worth it. But it takes courage to take one's life.'

The organising ability of the internees quickly emerged when it came to fitting the motley crowd into the available living-space.

'We were all taken to a hall. A lady there was allocating accommodation', says Dr H. 'On the boat a lady had recognised me from Vienna; she had been a patient in the hospital where I worked. She came with me to the lady who was doing the allocation and we were allotted a little house with a double bed. My new acquaintance said, "This is a doctor from Vienna. She couldn't share a double bed with me!" The lady came up to me and said, "I am a professional woman too." We both belonged to the International Federation of University Women. She now sent us to the best hotel at Port Erin, where the three officials had been put up, and we walked there together. The owners of the hotel said that they had only been told two days before about when we were actually coming. They said, "Choose a room", then we would have dinner. I said, "No, I want a bath first".

'I chose a room for myself. They asked me to help allocate the rooms for the second lot, expected the next day. I was a good organiser. I said, "Give me a list of the rooms", and I looked at them all. Next day, I was sitting downstairs, allocating rooms. I tried to give the refugees with children the best rooms. I kept the very best two rooms for an emergency. There was a lady in the hall with two children. She was crying. I rushed down and gave her a beautiful corner-room with three windows. She was away from her husband for the first time. She has stayed a faithful friend ever since.'

'We got to the Isle of Man', Freda says. 'There were two villages there, Port St Mary and Port Erin. We were allotted four to a room, and mostly people – complete strangers – had to share double beds. I was lucky: because I was pregnant I was allowed a bed to myself. I went out of the hotel and there was a fruit-shop opposite. And there were apples and I had not one halfpenny. My tears were flowing down. I could do nothing about it. Someone pressed sixpence into my hand. I walked into the shop and all I said was "Apples please." I got change as well. Never has anything tasted as good.'

Freda was not together with Marie Neurath now. Marie writes, 'We went by train through the beautiful island. At the station were people who selected us. A Scottish couple from Glasgow had the house, Ailsa Craig: most of us in it were from Holland and we all stuck together . . . .'

A song written for a festive occasion at Ailsa Craig gives some idea of the atmosphere of the time:

I

In Ailsa Craig there was a couple,
Quite happy and alone.
There was no noise, there was no trouble
There was no gramophone.
There was no roll-call folly,
No dust was on the floor,
There only was the parrot, Polly
And Nettle at the door, at the door.

II

But suddenly a big invasion –
It was a summer day –
Arrivèd at the railway station
And came from Holloway.
They came with empty belly
And full of thirst for life,
They swallowed bread and meat and jelly,
And numbered twenty-five, twenty-five.

III

The twenty-five had to be fixed
In rooms of two and three,
But these and those must not be mixed,
And others want to be.
When all were satisfièd,
Each one went to her bed,
But in the very deepest night
One from her bedroom fled, bedroom fled.

IV

And after that there was arranged
A single room for snore,
But this arrangement must be changed,
Not once, but twice and more.
The walls had no resistance,
The floor began to trill,
But thanks to heaven, in some distance,
Was hotel Peverill, Peverill.

V

But Peverill was not sufficient
For each catastrophe,
The kitchen girls were not efficient
Though they were served coffee.
They broke the plates in scores,
Cup vanished after cup,
And later some were found in drawers
And three behind the tub, 'hind the tub.

VI

Behind the tub and on the stair,
Was dirty every hole,
But not was there the brassière;
That was among the coal.
To show them off their habits,
Herself she cleaned the stair,
He could not help, for hunting rabbits
Took all his time to spare, time to spare.

VII

She rubbed and worked and round she looked,
No lazy-bone had chance,
She did the shopping and she cooked,
And went to airforce dance.
She cared for double heating,
For baths at every night
And at the house's general meeting
Was asked 'more light, more light, light, more light'.

VIII

But wait, in 1977
The trouble will be gone,
Our couple gets reward from heaven
For all that they have done.
They have their boiling kettle,
For coffees and for teas,
And have of Polly and of Nettle
The grandson and the niece, and the niece.

The need for organisation was obvious. Apart from anything else, many people (including the Dutch contingent) had no clothes. There were clothes collections. 'I dressed them from top to bottom' said Dr H. 'I got quite nice dresses', Marie Neurath agrees.

'On one of the first days', Dr H. told me, 'when the whole of the road had come down to the hotel and all the women wanted to talk to the commandant – most of them were without their husbands; some had even had to leave their children behind; they had had no news for about five weeks; and they were desperate – I had a brainwave. I said, "The commandant cannot talk to all of you. Elect a representative for every house. Tell her all your worries and then she will come with all your worries and we will have a meeting.'

'And we had meetings. I had a very efficient secretary next to me and she had to write down everything, and then we asked the commandant to come to meet us and we read our report out to her in English.'

The council included Marie Neurath: 'When we came into the house, there was a couple who looked after the house, and they said, "You should elect a representative." So Lucy Golombiewsky called out, "Longbein" – Long Legs – and that was me.'

The duties of the representative were varied. 'One thing we had to do was organise the work routine', said Marie Neurath. 'It was easy to get cooks', Dr H. added, 'because our hotel, the Hydro, was a big house and you just had to ask. We had a lot of domestics. One of the Austrian girls was very devoted to me; she was the head cook. I used to say, "Who wants to do the cleaning? Who wants to clean the commandant's room?" The commandant had a maid of her own. Later, everybody received sixpence a day real money for work they did. When I refused to accept it, I was permitted to carry on voluntarily. I had an excellent woman for the laundry: she gave out the laundry and collected it. She was a non-Jew engaged to a Jew in Prague. She said, "I will wait for him." She married him after the war.

'One had to do the lavatories. I insisted that people took turns. One lady I knew was very desperate and she paid someone to do the lavatories for her.

'In the morning I had to make announcements: "Such and such a thing has been reported missing – has anyone found it?" Then I had a complaints box. It was anonymous. I had to sort this out: stealing, neighbours making too much noise, etc. They also put suggestions in it.

'I had to see that all the lights were out at nine in the evening – those poor people! I was responsible for this. I had to go round and see they were all out. One day I saw a light under someone's door; I told them to push cushions in front of the door so that I wouldn't see.'

Medical services were almost immediately required. 'There was a doctor for people who got ill', Edith Jacobus told me. 'A refugee doctor.' One such was Dr H. 'I was in charge of the whole hotel: 190 people with thirty children, and if there was a call I had to rush out.

'There was a lot of anxiety and depression, and I immediately handed these over to a very nice psychologist in the camp the moment I noticed they were not suffering from a physical disease. Because these people needed an hour a day treatment and I didn't have that sort of time. There were also people aged seventy interned. One woman and her daughter always came to me at impossible times. The daughter was very good to her mother. The mother couldn't adjust. Just a little psychotherapy was needed. But we had no suicides while I was there.'

'Mrs G. tried to go into the sea and kill herself', Marie Neurath interjected. 'She came back saying, "The waves don't want me." Her daughter-in-law came to me and said, "I can't cope." I went to the justice of the peace and said, "Here is the problem. What shall I do?" "Keep her under supervision", and then he arranged to send her to a mental hospital.'

'We started a hospital in a little house off the main road', Dr H. continued. 'It was only a surgery with a very nice nurse. We got the equipment. If I needed something medical, I just had to ask. There was a very sweet Irish medical officer for the Isle of Man who said, "If you want advice, I am there", but I had rarely to bother him.

'The diseases depended on the places where they were living and the food they were getting. There was a little bit of vitamin deficiency in the small houses. Some of them used nettles as vegetables. The owners of the small houses got an allowance and it was their decision how they used it.

'One girl, she was only sixteen, and she lived on the fourth floor, came rolling down the stairs one day in really extreme pain. I diagnosed gallstones and sent her to the medical officer, who sent her to hospital in Douglas at once.

'We had a wonderful midwife there from the interned German Deaconess order. She went from one pregnant woman to another every day. I remember one confinement during the night. I didn't hear a thing. They didn't call me till seven in the morning. Then I had to tell the commandant. She was very cross; "Why wasn't I told? I am a fully-trained sister." Then I took her to see the baby. It was beautifully clean and quiet in its cot. It was wonderful.

'There was, I remember, a day when I was in the little hospital and a woman came in with her daughter of eighteen. "I am very worried. My daughter has not had her period since she's been here." I sent the mother out and examined the girl. I said, "You are three months pregnant." She said, "It's impossible. I've been with a man only once." I said, "You will have to tell your mother." They were Germans and not Jews. I called the mother in and said very tactfully, "It's not an illness. Is she engaged?" "More or less." So I said, "So you'll have the baby early." The mother was very shocked.

'There was another interesting case we had. An odd woman in her late thirties came to the hospital one day with a tummy-ache. I examined her and said, "You are almost nine months pregnant." She said, "No, no, no! I have never been with a man." Even when she was on the delivery table, she still said she was not pregnant and had a fibroid. The nice midwife got it out of her that she was once with a man. It was the funniest case ever.'

Dr H. celebrated her birthday on the Isle of Man and received many drawings, paintings and poems from the children, and over a hundred little presents, mostly home-made.

Very soon, Rushen camp was buzzing with schemes, not least in importance a nursery school for the children, run by a highly qualified teacher. 'How did we start the activities? We had nothing to do', explains Marie Neurath. 'Some people just knitted all the time. Some played the piano or walked about: it was very beautiful there. I remember sitting on the cliffs. Then one day I met other people. There were two women from Hamburg and one of them had studied economics. She had an idea: "Let's start a service exchange." So many people there could do different things; one could cut hair, one could teach languages, some made ornaments from shells on the beach. We organised paper money to buy and sell with. We got support from the official administration: they allowed us real money to buy materials with – wood, leather, etc. I had to do this. I didn't like it because I was new to England and didn't understand shopping.'

Of course, not everybody chose to engage in productive activity: 'In the beginning there was a golf course', an internee says. 'My parents sent us our golf clubs and we played golf every day. I wouldn't have missed it for anything.'

It must have been reports such as these that caused Sir Annesley Somerville, MP for Windsor, to ask the Home Secretary on 6 June whether he considered it right that 'these persons should be kept in luxurious idleness at this time . . . and is he also aware that there is a very great deal of feeling on this matter in the country . . . ?'; or Sir J. Wardlaw-Milne, MP for Kidderminster, Worcestershire, to draw his attention to 'considerable public resentment at the fact that the alien women interned in the Isle of Man were fully provided for by the government in hotels and boarding-houses at a payment of twenty-one shillings a week and are to be provided with swimming-baths, tennis-courts and golf-links, while the wife of a private soldier in the army gets an allowance of seventeen shillings a week plus seven shillings deducted from her husband's pay?'

Sir John repudiated the suggestion that 'specially favourable conditions are being provided for women interned in the Isle of Man. . . . The place chosen for their internment was selected after consultation with the Island authorities, and not because of its amenities, but because it is most suitable for purposes of security. Payment must be made by the Government to those persons whose premises are being used for the internment of these women and for the provision of food and the rates fixed are the minimum required for these purposes.'

And indeed the life-style obtaining in the women's camps on the Island was not without deficiencies. The food, for example, was not always entirely satisfactory. For some of the internees this came as rather a shock. An internee tells the story of a woman at her table at the Tower 'whose husband was quite famous in the film world and she was very delicate and very charming. When we had our first meal there and she was given her portion of mince, she said, "I think I'll wait for the next course. . . . " "There is no next course", they said.' 'The meals were awful', Freda says. 'Always watery stew and kippers. I lost stones and stones.' 'There was nice, fresh food, but too little, and I was terribly hungry', Marie Neurath complains. 'I used to go into the baker and buy bread. In prison the food was not so good but at least filling.' On the other hand, 'We lived mainly on bread', Edith Jacobus told me. 'There was plenty of bread to eat, and starchy food, with the result that we got styes in our eyes and eczemas. We never saw butter or eggs; people who had money bought their own.' Which corroborates Freda's statement that 'There was a big difference between the "haves" and "have-nots". The "haves" could have a lovely time.' 'Some people had money', Marie Neurath says, 'but they had to deposit it and were only allowed five shillings a week from it. If they wanted something expensive, they had to come with an invoice.'

There were endless problems involving personal relationships. Inevitably conflict occurred between Nazis and anti-Nazis. 'At our house one table was more or less all Nazis who made anti-semitic remarks', Marie Neurath says. 'One day they were in the room and everyone was talking at the same time and they said, "Mein Gott, we are in a Judeschule!" They had been domestics and had had the choice of whether to stay in England or to go back to Germany.' 'There were always fights and rough words were said to each other,' Edith Jacobus recalls, 'Nazis against non-Nazis.'

But basically it was not just Nazis against anti-Nazis. 'If people hadn't bickered so much,' Freda says, 'it would have been fantastic. People complained and fought. Every day there were about twenty people fighting. There were fights, verbal and physical, between the women all the time, about nothing or about house-duties – because we had to do house-duties every day, like waiting at table. I was exempt because I was pregnant.' 'Women together are always terrible', an internee concludes. 'There was always jealousy; it was quite a natural phenomenon.'

And these were women who were separated from their menfolk. Freda recalls, 'We had the freedom of two villages and could wander round. No man was safe there. In our hotel there was an old man of seventy-five; he was the owner of the hotel. He was watched over by his daughter. When she went off one day the women rushed in to rape him. The women went on the fishing-boats to get men.

The men there, the native inhabitants, had the time of their lives. The women fought over men like hyenas.'

Conversely, Marie Neurath states, 'The whole situation created a rather Lesbian atmosphere.'

But all this paled to insignificance in comparison with the very real agonies of separation from their loved ones, intensified frequently by complete ignorance of their whereabouts. 'We still didn't know where our men were', Freda explains. 'We had such a tough old commandant. When we asked about them, she said, "There's a war on. Our soldiers' wives don't know where their men are, why should you?" Then, of course, there were the rumours: the men had gone, the men had been deported, the men had to go into the army. I was expecting a child. I was frantic.'

Marie Neurath puts it more into perspective: 'Separation from family of course often meant suffering. But how can one compare this to the humiliation, torture, slave work, killing, in the concentration camps. Even in prison I felt safe, escaped from the Gestapo.'

Communication was also minimal, heightening anxiety. Marie writes, 'We were allowed to write one letter from prison. I wrote to Otto Neurath; I can't remember if this letter ever reached him. I remember that Frau Goldschmidt wrote to Queen Wilhelmina of the Netherlands. During the first weeks on the Isle of Man there were, I think, no letters at all. After some time blackboards were set up on which the names were written of those for whom letters had arrived. There was at first no postal connection from camp to camp. That came later.'

# 10 Their Finest Hour

The June weeks that saw the end of the Dunkirk evacuation (4 June), Italy's declaration of war on Britain (10 June), the entry of German troops into Paris (14 June), and the signing of the Franco-German armistice (23 June) left Britain standing alone, the next and obvious candidate for Nazi conquest. It also witnessed the inevitable progress towards general internment of enemy aliens.

Hitler took the first step in his invasion programme when he began, on 5 June, a series of small-scale air-raids on Britain. For the first time since September 1939 the siren sounded over a wide area of the country.

Preparations to combat the expected invasion began throughout Britain. Road-blocks were put up, anti-tank devices constructed, signposts and all other means of identifying localities removed; the ringing of church bells was banned except to announce the onset of invasion; every British household received a government leaflet telling its members how to behave *If the Invader Comes*.

Churchill ended his broadcast to the nation on 23 June, 'Let us therefore brace ourselves to our duties: and so bear ourselves that if the British Empire and its Commonwealth last for a thousand years, men will still say, "This was their finest hour."'

In homes all over Britain, boarding-houses, rented rooms, hotels, 'C' grade enemy aliens sat on their packed suitcases and waited for the ring on the doorbell.

The atmosphere in the country was ripe for the announcement of general internment. Anti-alien measures multiplied. In the early days of June, Home Office orders considerably increased the number and size of protected areas. An area twenty miles deep was marked out down the East coast from the Wash to Hastings wherein no alien of either sex could reside or enter.

Local authorities were instructed to suspend every foreigner engaged in any branch of civil defence work. Many borough councils had already done this. In Southgate, not only aliens but also naturalised British subjects of enemy birth had been dismissed. Middlesex County Council denied them access to any premises it utilised for civil defence purposes. Members of Wembley Council criticised the employment of German Jewish nurses in its hospitals. On 14 June the *Jewish Chronicle* reported that all enemy aliens employed by London County Council had been dismissed and refugee nurses in its hospitals removed.

The War Office contributed its mite to the torrent of distrust. Orders were issued suspending the enlistment of Germans and Austrians into the British Army.

'Would it not be much better to intern all foreigners?' Major Sir Philip Colfox, MP for Dorset, Western, asked Sir John Anderson in the House of Commons on 20 June. 'In view of the fact that under 11,000 Germans and Austrians have been interned out of an estimated total of 60,000', added Seymour Cocks, would the Home Secretary take measures to make a further large reduction in the number still at liberty?

The House of Lords and the press felt the same. The *Evening News*, for example: 'The time to solve the enemy alien problem is now. And the only sure and safe solution is to intern all the male enemy aliens between sixteen and sixty at once.'

But still no announcement came, though on 31 May Chief Constables throughout the country received letters from the Home Office. They were now permitted to intern any German or Austrian, man or woman, in category 'C', where there were grounds for doubting their reliability, and the age-limit for internment was raised from sixty to seventy.

Equally, action was taken against the Italians. Italians in Britain were already objects of growing suspicion at the end of May. Would the Home Secretary 'consider reviewing the number of foreign waiters employed in restaurants and road-houses in the vicinity of important aerodromes and aircraft factories, and take action in this matter?' asked Major Sir Jocelyn Lucas, MP for Portsmouth, South, on 30 May. Would he, 'in the interest of public safety, have an inquiry made into the Savoy Hotel, which is staffed with anti-British Italians, seeing that highly placed officers frequently dine there?' echoed Ernest Thurtle (Shoreditch) on the same day.

When Mussolini declared war on Britain on 10 June a massive round-up of Italians in the country was already well under way. All Italian residents in Britain who were known to be members of the

Italian Fascist Party, except the invalid and infirm, and all other Italians between the ages of sixteen and seventy who had lived in the country for less than twenty years were ordered to be interned. They added up to a total of some 4100. Eugen Spier records the arrival at Lingfield racecourse of 'a series of charabancs loaded with hundreds of Italians many of whom were well known to me as managers, head waiters, waiters from London West End restaurants and from such places as the Savoy, Ritz, Berkeley, Hungaria, etc., together with many well-known figures from London's Soho district.'

But still no measure of general internment was announced. One can only assume that the shortage of accommodation which had already bothered Anderson in May was still a major concern. It is also legitimate to assume that the policy of deportation of some of those already in internment-camps was the government's answer to this problem of space.

As early as 3 June, a minute from that champion of democracy, Prime Minister Winston Churchill, asked his Cabinet Secretary, 'Has anything been done about shipping 20,000 internees to Newfoundland or St Helena? Is this one of the matters that the Lord President has in hand? If so, would you please ask him about it. I should like to get them on the high seas as soon as possible . . . .' The following day in the House of Commons, Walter Higgs, MP for Birmingham, West, asked the Secretary of State for War whether he would 'consider the desirability of transporting internees and prisoners of war to places remote from the British Isles in order to prevent co-operation with enemy aircraft and parachutists?' Would he bear in mind, chipped in another MP, Mr J. Henderson Stewart (MP for East Fife), 'the danger which may result from the landing of parachutists from German planes who may fall inside German camps in this country?'

Others, even more influential, were thinking on the same lines. On 7 June, Viscount Caldecote, Secretary of State for the Dominions, sent the following note to Vincent Massey, High Commissioner for the Canadian Government in London: 'The total number of German internees in this country is now over 12,000 of whom 2500 are definitely pro-Nazi in sympathy and allegiance and therefore a source of danger in the event, for example, of parachute landings or invasion of the country. . . . In the circumstances the United Kingdom Government sincerely hopes that the Canadian Government may be pressed to come to the assistance of the United Kingdom by agreeing to receive at the earliest possible moment, at least the internees whose removal from this country it is desired to secure on the ground that their continued presence in this country is bound to be a source of the most serious risk.'

On 19 June the Canadian Prime Minister, Mackenzie King, told Parliament that Canada was ready to take interned aliens and German prisoners of war from Great Britain. The action, he said, was being taken at the request of Great Britain because of the danger of having a potential enemy in the midst of the people during the threat of invasion.

In line with this thought-process, the Home Office reassured Bloomsbury House that it was intended at the moment only to remove from Britain prisoners of war and other enemy aliens who had been interned for special reasons and who might prove dangerous in certain circumstances.

Two days after the Canadian agreement, Alexander Maxwell wrote to Chief Constables throughout the country informing them that His Majesty's Government had decided to adopt a policy of interning, subject to certain exceptions, male Germans and Austrians now at large in Britain.

The connection seems obvious. It is strengthened by the schedule for the process of general internment. Because of accommodation problems it was to be carried out in three phases (and, even so, many of the female internees had to be lodged for considerable periods in Holloway prison until room could be found for them on the Isle of Man). The first phase, to begin on 25 June, was to involve all Germans and Austrians without refugee status, except those who had been in Britain for over twenty years, and all Germans and Austrians unemployed at that juncture. The second phase was to start on 4 July and to encompass all other Germans and Austrians outside London. The final phase, scheduled for 10 July, would sweep all remaining German and Austrian enemy aliens into internment-camps.

Ships carrying internees to the dominions sailed on 24 June and 1, 2, 4 and 10 July.

Osbert Peake later explained the criteria governing the selection of internees for deportation to Canada. First priority was obviously given to Nazi seamen who had been interned and who ranked as civilian internees. Then, in order of preference, came internees who had been interned for security purposes and single men in category 'B', particularly those who did not object to going. So far as possible, he assured the House of Commons, the most dangerous classes of

internees were to be sent to Canada, but, where it had been
necessary to make up numbers, single men under fifty had been
chosen, and, in preference, those who expressed a wish to go. The
Italians included were those who had been interned for security
reasons.

Australia had also expressed her willingness to receive not only
men but also women and children, thus opening up the possibility of
reuniting families.

Some of the subtleties of selection emerge from individual cases.
Sir Edward Grigg in September told of one Professor Pringsheim
and his four sons. The Professor and the three eldest were interned in
the Central Promenade camp; the youngest was in Onchan camp.
The three eldest were sent overseas on a general order to send all
single men between the ages of twenty and thirty. They sailed on the
steamship *Ettrick* on 2 July. The youngest son did not go with them
because the lower age-limit was then twenty. For the next
steamship, the *Sobieski*, which sailed on 4 July, the age-limit for
single men had been lowered to sixteen in order to send as few
married men as possible. The youngest was embarked on this ship.

When the first such ship, the 20,000-ton *Duchess of York*, owned by
the Canadian Pacific Steamship Company, left Liverpool docks,
Eugen Spier was on board. He was convinced until the last moment
that he was going to join his wife on the Isle of Man. When the size of
the vessel and the name of its owner stamped on his ticket forced
realisation upon him, he awoke to its full implications. 'Cut off from
England, from home, without any possible contact with my wife
and son, who knew nothing of my whereabouts and my fate, nor had
I any knowledge of theirs . . . This was a terrible prospect.'

Spier had not been given the choice of staying in England, had
not even been told beforehand that he was being sent abroad. In the
days following the sailing of the *Duchess of York*, an attempt was
made to persuade internees to opt for deportation. Chaim Rabin,
for example, remembers, 'The camp administration was putting it
about that we were all going to Australia. It was therefore worth our
while to volunteer to go because as volunteers we would be better
treated. There was a lot of propaganda for it. We always felt that we
were going to be betrayed and therefore when the Australian
proposal came along, we did not trust it. One person was put in
charge of the Australian registration. We all hated him and called
him the deportation officer.'

Another internee reports, 'They said, "You are all going

overseas. You can go now or when the situation gets worse." So I said I would go now.'

Felix Darnbacher remembers being faced with a similar decision: 'People were being sent to Canada. One transport was going. If you volunteered to go, they promised they would release you there, and your near and dear ones would be sent on. A British officer in khaki stood up and said this. We volunteered . . . .'

So too did Klaus Loewald: 'When it was announced that a transport was to leave Liverpool and that volunteers were welcome,' he writes, 'the internees split into groups of those who wished to go, since they feared, just as did the British, an invasion by Hitler, from whom they had more or less recently fled, and of those who wanted to stay in England because the presence there of their families or the advanced state of their preparations to migrate across the Atlantic outweighed their fear of a German onslaught.

'Our group was both eager to go and fearful that one or the other of its members might be rejected or not needed. When volunteering, therefore, we concocted an elaborate scheme under which we represented ourselves as reasonably close relatives who wished to remain together. We need not have feared. Many internees were forced to embark because the number of volunteers was too small.'

Jakob Felsenstein, on the other hand, had made up his mind in advance: 'I had previously arranged with my wife (who was technically German since she had married me) that in view of the danger of Britain being invaded, she should get herself interned as well, and we would both opt to get sent abroad – which to us meant Canada, and we had family there. In Huyton, there was an announcement calling for volunteers to go abroad. I wouldn't have had to go because I was married. We were told we would be given a much greater degree of freedom in the "dominion" to which we would be sent, we would be allowed to work, etc. And they also said that our wives would be allowed to join us.'

In the event, no women were shipped overseas in fulfilment of this alleged promise, though various attempts were said to have been made to carry it out.

Erich Mark also seems to have been given an element of choice: 'Together with some other internees, I applied to go to the Isle of Man, rather than Australia, for two reasons: distance from my family; and the suspicion that the real Germans were being sent as far as possible from England. The only reason for not preferring the Isle of Man was the thought that the Germans might invade Ireland first and then cross the Irish Sea, getting to us first.'

As the results of persuasion were not entirely overwhelming, selection was again adopted as a means of choosing candidates for deportation. Peter Katz, for example, says, 'In July they started deportation. Lists were drawn up by the elders of the camp in conjunction with the commandant. Each camp had to provide a quota. Some people were quite pleased to go. I didn't want to go because I had my parents in London.'

'Some people were willing to pay not to have to go', Leon Feldman adds. 'They used to say, "You are my stand-in in case I'm chosen", or "I want to go to Canada, you want to go to Australia". The rumours came round that it was "only single men" or "only married men".'

'One day', Martin Ostwald told me, 'came the order that everyone who was under forty or over eighteen and unmarried should report. Rumours began to fly about what was going to happen to us, including one which proved correct that we were going to be shipped to Canada. I remember one old man of about sixty who switched places because he had a son in Cuba.'

'On about 3 July', Moses Aberbach remembers, 'a large number of people in the camp were told that they would be leaving for Canada. I was supposed to be among them. At four o'clock in the morning they went on board ship. At eleven o'clock the previous night Dr Van der Zyl had come and told me that my release papers had arrived and I was not to go to Canada.' On 5 July he was home with his parents.

# 11 Porridge-chutists

Chief Constables duly began their task on 25 June. The *Jewish Chronicle* that week reported that widespread arrests among category 'C' refugees had taken place in the early hours of the morning. Most were in North-West and South-West London, and in Manchester, Leeds and Sheffield. From Manchester came the news that Rabbi Dr Moritz David (formerly of Bochum, Germany) was one of the eight male refugees resident in the Refugee Annexe to the Homes for Aged and Needy Jews in Cheetham Hill Road who had been interned.

Rudi Guttman was also taken during this phase. He had been sent to school in England (the Regent's Park School for German-Jewish children run by Mrs George Schindler) by a prescient father in January 1934. His engineering studies were interrupted by the war and his many attempts to join the armed services were rejected. July 1940 found him unemployed.

'I had been to a tribunal in 1939 in Deal, Kent – the school had been on holiday there at the start of the war and did not go back to London. I was classed as a friendly enemy alien.

'On 1 July 1940 I had to report to the police-station between Great Portland Street tube-station and Oxford Street [Albany Street?]. I was told to bring a suitcase with clothes. From there, I was taken by bus, truck, or something to Lingfield. We slept in stables there. It was no hardship for me because we were young.'

At Lingfield, Guttman met an old school-friend, Erich Mark.

'When the Nazi May offensive began in the Netherlands,' Mark writes, 'I was not yet eighteen and had been working for about eighteen months in a firm producing briar pipes and other consumer articles in Hammersmith. I was living with a Jewish family with a son and a daughter of about my own age in West Kensington. My parents had been unable to leave Germany.

'In May the first reports of possible mass internment of "enemy aliens" had been printed in the newspapers and I was not altogether

63

surprised to find two policemen at the house at about 7 a.m. one morning in June, one in uniform, who asked me to pack my bags. I was told it might only be for a few days, and indeed we had heard of protests made in Parliament about the lack of selectivity, putting real Nazis together with refugees from Germany.

'The police were pleasant enough, and I spent that day and the night at Hammersmith police-station, my first experience of the inside of a cell. Next day we – all men – were taken by coach to Lingfield racecourse on the borders of Surrey and Sussex. The weather was perfect, the countryside beautiful and for me it was something of an adventure, because I just could not believe the mistake would not be recognised quickly.

'At the racecourse we were gradually sorted out into groups that would share sleeping accommodation in the stables, and the main concern of some of my fellow internees was not to get into the same stable as some presumed Nazis. Life was unwontedly lazy and that took some getting used to, especially as idle moments tended to reinforce the spreading of rumours – we did not at first get newspapers or radio.

'On the second or third day I volunteered to do some work and promptly found myself doing the most menial job going: washing up in the kitchen. Arrangements were very primitive at first; we had no washing-powder, but gradually managed to get hold of soda and even hot water, which made the job quite bearable. In any case the advantage was that the cooks favoured the washers-up with extra rations! The weather continued fine, there was the fascination of being in an all-male society made up of very varied talents and levels of culture. Not very long after we got to Lingfield the first cultural evening was organised, mainly musical, and there was some participation by the troops guarding us, though I don't remember details. What has remained clearly in mind was a most beautiful performance of Beethoven's Moonlight Sonata sitting on the stands of the racecourse, bathed in full moonlight.

'After that, the atmosphere became rather more tense because transports were being assembled for the Isle of Man and Australia, and there was a report that one of the latter had been torpedoed. One of my school-friends, who had come to Lingfield at about the same time as I, was sent off.'

Felix Darnbacher had been at Mrs Schindler's school since he was thirteen years old, in 1933. In his case, however, his parents were able to follow him to England, and in 1940 the family was living together in Highbury New Park, London.

'On 27 June a policeman came along and said, "Look, I have to intern you. Come to the police-station tomorrow. Bring enough stuff for twenty-four hours." My father was sufficiently experienced. He packed two little cases and took all his cash. He put it in a body-belt – romantic, spy-story stuff. Next day, we travelled peaceably to the police-station at the requisite hour (we should have gone on holiday as so many people did). That was the first time I was locked up in a cell. It was a very terrifying experience, hearing the door clang and knowing you really cannot move. Other people gradually accumulated and then we were all sent on a lorry to Kempton Park.

'There was barbed wire all round the place and guards marching up and down. It was a typical British muddle: kindly disorganisation. Food was very sparse because of the muddle and no one knew anything.'

Frankfurt-born Chaim Rabin, who had come to England from Palestine to study Hebrew and Arabic, was also taken to Kempton Park.

'I think I was expecting to be interned. I had Arabic books to work on. I only heard of one case in Golders Green where the family had protested; most of us took it quite calmly. This was a religious family in Golders Green where the wife and children had all started wailing when the police came to take the husband away. The police left and the family wasn't interned.

'So we were taken to a police-station. They put down my name and we were taken to Kempton Park. It was a complete *balagan* [confusion]. Conditions were very primitive and we slept in stables on palliasses. We had nothing to do. The soldiers who guarded us had just come back from Dunkirk and had been told that we were German prisoners of war. They refrained from talking to us. We had Neville Chamberlain's dentist with us. He had been in England for years, spoke beautiful English and looked very much like an Englishman. He asked the soldiers, "Who do you think we are?" "Parachutists." He pointed to the old rabbis with their flowing beards and *payot* [side-curls], and asked, "Do they look like parachutists?" "Yes, of course. They are disguised." After that, they called us "Porridge-chutists", because we were fed largely on porridge. They'd told them all this about us because they wanted them to keep a good watch on us.

'Then we were taken to Huyton near Liverpool.'

Klaus Loewald was living with a family of refugees who had been neighbours in Berlin, and was working in a small factory. He writes, 'I even had twenty-four hours' warning. One day, while at work, I was called to the telephone to be informed that my host and his elder son, aged eighteen, had been interned that morning after I had left for my place of employment, that the police had inquired after me, and that I was requested kindly to stay at home the next day so as to enable them to pick me up.

'I was delighted. My permission to live in England was contingent on my continuing and perfecting my training; the position, while badly paid and without future, was the means by which I had been saved from Germany, and I was conscious of, and grateful for, it, while at the same time feeling trapped. Internment was a way out. Moreover, I was very young for my nineteen years and excited by what appeared to be a stimulating new development. I bid farewell to my employers and fellow workers after completing the entire working day at the shop, went home, and packed a small suitcase.

'In the morning of 28 June 1940, I was interned by a polite official who, amazed not only that I had waited for him but that I was ready to accompany him with a packed suitcase, felt sufficiently overcome to enter the flat and accept a cup of tea. He then took me to the Black Maria, picked up one or two other refugees, and deposited us at what I believe is the Brompton Oratory. Soon afterwards, possibly on the same day, we were taken to a camp on Kempton Park racecourse.'

# 12 Huyton

'This is the only one instance in which a housing-estate is being used for the accommodation of aliens', the Secretary of State for War told the House of Commons on 30 May. 'And this', he added, 'is only a temporary arrangement pending transfer to a permanent camp.' The housing-estate was at Huyton near Liverpool. It was brought into use as an internment-camp when general internment policy began in May 1940. For thousands of internees it was the jumping-off point for the Isle of Man or the Dominions. Some spent the major portion of their internment there. It was still occupied in spring 1941.

Both Ulrich Skaller and Martin Ostwald were amongst the first occupants. Skaller told me, 'At Huyton we disembarked and had to wait for about twenty minutes on the station platform. At the other platform a train arrived, and again hundreds of people disembarked. One of our group said, "Let's look over there and see whether there are some of our acquaintances." And suddenly someone waved madly at me: it was my cousin, Frederick Skaller.

'From Huyton station we marched to the camp, which I think was still uninhabited. I think we even got bedsteads there – palliasses on bedsteads. The food was not as good as at Warley but it was passable. But one evening a very big transport of internees arrived for which the camp was not prepared, and, as a consequence, the meals for one day were very scanty. The commandant was a very old colonel who spent his time in organising his little troop of guards. He would surround a house and storm it.'

Ostwald was also in the first batch: 'We were put into uninhabited unfurnished houses. We were given sacks and had to stuff them to make palliasses. In Huyton Freddy Grunfeld composed our own song, which spread all over the camps:

You'll get used to it
The first year is the worst year, then you'll get used to it.
You can scream and you can shout,
They will never let you out!
It serves you right, you so-and-so,
Why weren't you a naturalised Eskimo?
It's marvellous, it's wonderful,
You'll get to like it more and more and more.
And once you get used to it,
And when you get used to it,
You feel just as lousy as you felt before.

By the beginning of June there were about 2500 men at Huyton. In the middle of July, *Reynolds News* published a letter from an inmate: 'The camp is a disgrace. There is no material for cleaning. Each person has a palliasse and three blankets. There are no tables and no chairs. Food is quite inadequate . . . there have been two suicides in one week. . . . There is a lack of even the most primitive medical supplies. It is essential that an impartial Englishman should look into the matter, which is a barbaric disgrace. After being put into category "C" we are now treated worse than prisoners of war. It takes eight to ten days to get a sheet of notepaper. . . . The canteen charges fabulous prices. Newspapers can only be obtained through unofficial channels and at prices to match, and so rumourmongers have their way with us.'

It must have been around this time that Chaim Rabin was taken to Huyton: 'I was very lucky: I was put into a house that became the post-office. I therefore became a worker, which was definitely an advantage. The other great advantage was that, because it was an office, we got tables and chairs. I was the man who carried the mail from the main camp to the branch camps. People were allowed to have as much post as arrived. The outgoing mail had to be on special paper and this was in very short supply. It was discovered in the first few days that the only man in England who could produce it had also been interned! He was let out very quickly.'

Mail was, as we have seen, a continual problem, a constant source of complaint and recrimination. Ulrich Skaller remembers, 'When I was a month there and one was allowed to communicate I asked for permission to send a telegram to my wife. The next day I was told that permission was refused and I was given my money back. Nevertheless the telegram arrived, stating, "Address 65 Hillside

Road AIC Camp Huyton." Then we were allowed once a week a letter.'

The exigencies of the postal service caused Pastor Ehrhardt to compose the following verse:

> There was once a postman at Huyton
> Whom the glittering bayonets did frighten.
> So he hopped it for good,
> And delivered all food,
> All parcels and letters at Brighton!

His wife remembers that the censors asked certain men to tell their relatives to write in German, as they couldn't understand the dictionary 'English' (known as 'Emigranto').

There were advantages to being a worker. Batya Emanuel recalls that, 'when they talked about deporting people to Australia or Canada, my father did everything to keep my brothers with him, because he said that we had had to leave all our wealth in Germany but our biggest treasure we had taken with us, our five children. So he got my brother to work in the kitchen because people who had jobs were often not transported.'

But this was not the only benefit. Chaim Rabin continues, 'People who worked were very well treated. They not only got money (I came back with thirty shillings in my account); they also got milk and half a pound of cheese a week. Then they set up a special shop; only those who worked could buy in it with tokens, and therefore we got more extra food. A boy in our house worked in the kitchens and he could take stuff back with him. For *Rosh Hashanah*, he requisitioned lots of stuff and we had a lovely meal. I can't remember how we cooked it because there were no stoves in the houses, only bath-stoves that heated the water with wood. Some people earned money collecting wood and letting others have baths in their houses. There were all kinds of ingenious ways of making money. One chap set up an office with a table and advised people how to go to Brazil. Some people got quite rich. One group opened a café in one of the nice parts of the camp and got tables from the camp-management. They served coffee with whipped cream, and little cakes. It was quite famous, this café, and the officers used to come and have coffee there.

'One man, a very academic looking fellow, collected herrings and built his own stove. He smoked the fish and sold them as buckling.

There were a lot of herrings available because the Navy had captured a German ship and, as English people don't eat herrings, we were given them completely raw, straight from the barrel.

'The food at first was awful because they handed the food to the inmates and said, "Cook it yourselves." No one knew how to cook. Then, they moved in groups of army cooks and the food suddenly got very good, except in the kosher part. I admit with regret that I wasn't there. The koshers cooked for themselves. They got their kosher meat (and also *siddurim* [prayer-books]) from the rabbinate.'

Batya Emanuel corroborates the deficiencies of the kosher food: 'My father lost a lot of weight. He was so thin, he was just a skeleton. We used to send him parcels with kosher food because they had such poor food and they couldn't eat most of the things. We were very poor but my mother made cakes and sent them.'

Huyton was organised very early on to cater for the needs of the orthodox Jews constrained to live there. By early June, when the Chief Rabbi called on the War Office in connection with the religious requirements of internees, and the authorities 'kindly' promised to give facilities for kosher kitchens in camps as soon as possible, the *Jewish Chronicle* could report that in Huyton the necessary steps had already been taken. Visits by outside rabbis were also permitted. Rabbi Dr S. M. Lehrman tells of one such occasion: 'The commandant was very nice and very obliging. He asked one of his lieutenants to take me round. He said, "I have four rabbis here." I went to see them. They were all in one room and two of them were ill, lying on palliasses on the floor. I got them at once into a bedroom; I saw to it myself. The next time I went I saw that the rabbis were much better; they had beds. I visited Huyton once a month. There were a lot of students there. The Liverpool Jewish community gave them a *Sefer Torah* [Scroll of the Law]. If they had any difficulty, they came to me.'

A reflection too of the hungry early period is Pastor Ehrhardt's limerick which also records the continuous letter-writing activity by the internees in attempts to obtain release:

> There is also a 'C' case from Ealing,
> Quite nosey, rather appealing.
> He is writing with zeal,
> His daily appeal,
> To prevent that queer sinking feeling.

However, the treatment, Rabin feels, was good. 'There were big circular tents and houses in Huyton', says another internee. 'The houses were for older people. I was taken to a tent. The people there who were in tents, and usually young, got the feeling that the whole thing was a bit of a lark.' 'The supervision', according to Rabin, 'consisted only of the morning and evening roll-calls and otherwise they didn't interfere with us – except for the barbed wire.'

The barbed wire caused difficulties of its own. Moses Aberbach recalls, 'There were orthodox Jews there who as usual had a *halachic* [Jewish religious law] problem: "Is it permitted to carry things within the camp on the Sabbath?" They decided that it was only permitted if the barbed wire around the camp belonged to the Jewish inmates. They sent a delegation of three to ask the camp commandant to sell the barbed wire to them for one shilling. The camp commandant suspected the worst. He probably thought that the Jews were trying to buy it as some devious means to escape. He threw them out. They came back twice and then three times to try to explain but he refused to listen.'

'I think one or two people did try to escape', Rabin remembers, 'but they didn't get very far. But once some transports were taken to another camp. The internees were taken to the station and lined up on the platform. The people asked to go to the WC. When they came out, the column had moved on. They tried to join it, but a policeman said, "No. These are prisoners." So they went out and had a meal and a good time. They still had some money – this was before camp money was introduced. When their money ran out, they went back to Huyton. The guard at the gate said, "You can't come in. This is an internment-camp." But an officer recognised them and they were let in.

'At the time we were living in tents, one tent contained the list of people and of categories filed on red cards. One group volunteered to work in this tent. They had been clerks and were non-Jewish Germans. They were very keen to get the lists into their hands. We had a lot of difficulty trying to get this group out. Then a camp representation was set up, with a number of people representing the inmates of the camp. Some of us got together and went to the commandant. We asked that the Nazis be taken out. They were people who spied on us. The commandant said, "We can't put them out. Are they represented on your council? They are a separate group and should be represented." When we were taken to the Isle of Man the Nazis remained behind, therefore it did have some effect.

'The wife of one man was having a baby and he said could he go home to be with her while she was having it. He went to the camp commandant, who answered, "You know, my wife is also having a baby and I haven't even applied for leave!" There was a cultural gap there.

'There were different attitudes amongst the internees too. Some people were worried about their wives and families; some just accepted it. Some were very glad that their wives and families were being kept by the government; these were the people who'd applied for emigration. Some didn't apply for release at all; they were the ones who wanted to have a mixed camp on the Isle of Man. There were also other groups. Next to us, there were a few houses of elderly Jews from Galicia who had been interned from Manchester. They had never applied for naturalisation. They were very happy; they used to sit there playing cards all day. They didn't want to get out. Then one of them was let out; he gave an interview to the *Manchester Guardian* saying that the conditions were excellent. It was like a good holiday resort. He would like to go back. This created an uproar amongst the refugees.

'There was a high percentage of intellectuals there. There was the man who had been the professor of philosophy at Berlin, Lieber. He had already retired. He addressed everyone as "Herr Dr", and everyone who looked the least bit intellectual as "Herr Professor". I taught a course on "The History of Zionism", and also Hebrew and Arabic. The only notes you could take were on toilet-paper; someone brought home a whole history of Zionism on toilet-paper. There were all sorts of lectures. There was one man, a Dr Regensburger, who started in the morning at five o'clock to go to a class in *Tenach* [the Jewish Bible] and went on attending lectures until ten at night. He made himself extra pockets in his jackets so that he could carry his books around. He had been a judge in Germany and had had a very large library. Someone in the camp command suggested that he should bring his library to the camp but the store where the books were kept was bombed.'

None the less, a library was opened at Huyton. Skaller found it a godsend: 'People sent some books (the Red Cross, the Quakers, Jewish organisations) and it was quite substantial. When I went once or twice to the library and got talking to the librarian, he said, "Why don't you come and help me?" and I took over for two days a week. It was done in turns; there were about six of us.' The Chief Rabbi's Religious Emergency Council, an advisory committee for the religious welfare of internees, was early on publishing appeals for gifts of books in the *Jewish Chronicle*, in order to supply 'the religious and cultural needs of our interned brethren'.

Skaller saw other aspects of culture at Huyton: 'We had, I think, daily voluntary English lessons given by those internees who spoke better than others. We played a lot of chess and there were some excellent chess-players there, some former minor German chess-masters, who gave us handicaps. They played us only with one castle and beat us. There were theatre performances staged. One of my co-internees was Landauer (of Ravicz and Landauer) and he did musical arrangements and took songs from old operettas and put on performances. It was marvellous, given the circumstances. The English officers gave us great applause. They were also very bored and for them it was as great an entertainment as for us.'

Culture was not the only preoccupation. Amongst the internees were many young Zionists filled with the ideal of the value of working with their hands and wanting only to proceed to Palestine to work its ungrateful soil by the sweat of their brows. Rabin writes, 'We had a shoemaker's shop and a lot of these people worked in it as a way of retraining themselves. There was one real shoemaker from the East End of London and they looked down on him. He complained about it.

'There were all kinds of societies. I was invited by the Zionist Society to speak about possibilities of employment in Palestine. As most of them were intellectuals, I said that, once the war was finished, there would be a great need for intellectuals and everyone should learn Hebrew and then find work there. They were very angry: they said they wanted to do manual work there.

'I learned to lecture there; I lectured about twice a week. I was quite young then, twenty-five, and completely unprepared. There were hardly any books there. There were huts where we could meet but they did not have blackout and there were raids and bombardments going on all the time. I had to be so interesting that I could keep the old people from running out. I learned to be interesting. I should pay the British government for this: when I came out I could talk at the word "go".

'There was at that time a feeling that we were being cheated on all sorts of things. We felt that if the Germans came we'd be handed over to them. We made all sorts of plans to break out if they did come. This was one of the worst aspects, this fear of something worse.'

This fear was nourished by the ban on ownership of radios or newspapers, the absence in fact of all news from the outside world. Skaller remembers that 'some people were terribly pessimistic and said, "the day after tomorrow the Germans will be here" '. The lack of understanding in official circles of the special fear of a German invasion felt by German Jews is typified by Sir Edward Grigg's comment in Parliament on 10 July: 'The people in the internment-camps are in no more danger from parachutists and so on than those in English schools . . . .' It was not until the latter half of July that Josiah Wedgwood (MP for Newcastle under Lyme) asked the Prime Minister in the House 'whether he could give the pledge of His Majesty's Government that alien refugees from Hitler, now interned in this country, would in no circumstances be handed back to Hitler, as in France'. 'Yes, Sir', Winston Churchill replied. 'It is inconceivable to me that His Majesty's Government, either now or at any future date, would hand over to their oppressors persons who had sought in this country a refuge from persecution.'

Pastor Ehrhardt told his wife of this fear. She writes, 'My husband told afterwards that there was considerable nervousness when it was learned that the Vichy government in France had handed their internment-camps intact to the Gestapo, so he told them that certain of the guards were Communists and had promised to open the gates in time for everybody to get to any ships there might be in Liverpool. To which a German Communist said, "And that's supposed to be a parson!" '

In camp at this period, writer Stefan Pollatschek made notes for a story, which he never wrote, based on an invasion by Hitler of the British Isles. It reaches a climax with the assassination of the head of the Gestapo in London, followed by punitive action by 5000 German aircraft devastating Britain and the deportation of all survivors to the East. The notes continue, 'There is no doubt that the English reader of these lines will take them as the deranged fantasy of a refugee (bloody foreigner). He will not believe them . . . .

'It is possible that the refugee (bloody foreigner) has no idea what fair play is. But he has more than an idea what Hitler is.

'Fair play? Yes. But only after Hitler has been conquered.'

Visits from close relatives were permitted later on. Batya Emanuel remembers, 'My mother got permission for both of us to visit my father and you also needed permission to enter the area as it was by the sea. When you came to the camp there was a certain hut where visitors were received. Here, an acquaintance brought us hot coffee and sat down with us. After a while, one of the soldiers said, "I think these are Emanuel's visitors, not yours." We were told when it was time to go, and on the way to the exit, several of the men asked me to pass messages on to their wives, and gave me their telephone-numbers, to tell them that next day they were being shipped to the Isle of Man.'

Skaller says, 'One day we were told that there was also an internment-camp on the Isle of Man and there would be proper facilities for kosher food there and whoever wanted to go there for this reason could go. But I knew that by then efforts were being made to get me released and I thought that if I changed my residence I would only delay things.'

Rabin opted to move: 'When we left Huyton we did our utmost to dirty our rooms. We did as much as possible to leave the place in a bad state.'

Rabbi Lehrmann remembers another farewell: 'Then came the day when a lot of them were taken to Australia. I was asked to come along and say goodbye. They were all lined up. It was pouring with rain. I had an umbrella. I said goodbye to each personally and shook their hands.'

Pastor Ehrhardt summed up his impressions of Huyton in a scholarly article he later wrote entitled 'The Birth of the Synagogue and Rabbi Akiba': 'At all these various places something happened, which I myself was able to observe at the internment in 1940. Under conditions of grim asperity, under canvas, with insufficient food, the interned refugees developed at once an active, responsible adminis-tration. Men of recognised learning were put in charge, for scholarship was the only distinction that was generally recognised. Prince Frederick of Prussia, despite his family connections with Queen Mary, was not found a place in it; neither did great wealth receive any consideration. This administration set itself three tasks: first, the registration of everybody present, so that not a single case of distress should go unnoticed; second, the organisation of assistance for the old, the sick and the destitute; and, third, the satisfaction of cultural demands through libraries, schools, lectures, etc. The general improvement of material conditions at the camp lagged a long way behind.'

# 13 The Isle of Men (I)

The Isle of Man eventually became the main internment centre for those detained in Britain. Internees were brought from all the other camps and many of these were closed down or used for different purposes.

Apart from the women's camps at Port Erin and Port St Mary, several men's camps were opened on the island. Owners of boarding-houses at the seaside resorts of Onchan and Ramsey were the first to receive the dreaded letter from the War Office on 12 May, ordering them to vacate their premises, leaving behind them their whole stock in trade: furniture, bedding, linen, cutlery, crockery and utensils. Their joy knew no bounds!

The new occupants were brought to the Isle of Man via Liverpool and the journey thither was not always the most pleasant experience. In fact, any movement through a public thoroughfare could arouse hostile reaction from the populace.

A not untypical example was given by a doctor of international law, writing in the *Jewish Chronicle* on 13 September 1940: 'On the way, we were addressed by the Lieutenant as "prisoners of war". The manner in which we marched through villages was such that onlookers must have had the impression that we were either prisoners of war or parachutists. As a matter of fact I was asked by a lady "Where I had jumped?" Which inquiry I answered by saying "from a bus". While marching we sang to the tune of the British National Anthem "We are refugees; thanks for your hospitality", just in order to inform the onlookers that we had nothing to do with Hitlerism.'

Leon Feldman had a similar experience: 'To get to the Isle of Man, we had to pass through Liverpool. We had to march through the streets to the port. The people were really nasty. We had to march through a narrow cordon of guards with mounted bayonets. This was awful.

'We were put up in various hotels on the island. They had put barbed wire on beaches – where did they think we were going to swim to? Immediately the rumour factory began. What was happening in the war? Why was there such a lot of air activity? All single men were to be transported to Canada and Australia.'

As far as Feldman was concerned, this latter rumour proved correct; so too in the case of Martin Ostwald. Both had left the island by the early days of July. Ostwald writes, 'I was in Douglas in a boarding-house on the waterfront. The street in front of the houses was as wide as a room and then, directly in front, was barbed wire. We were two or three to a room. The places were sparsely decorated but quite comfortable. Everybody who knew something gave lectures and everyone who had a book shared it. There was a schoolmaster who made us write essays in English. The camp spokesman was non-Jewish, he was Count Lingen, the Kaiser's grandson and he had been at Cambridge.'

The young schoolboy Peter Katz was brought from Warth Mill in the middle of June and stayed somewhat longer: 'We went to Onchan camp, a couple of miles above Douglas, on a hill – a beautiful location. I would think that Onchan was the best camp in the United Kingdom. It actually had a playing-field, a full-size football pitch. On the way to Onchan we marched past Douglas and past an Italian internment camp at Douglas, and they looked terribly caged-in with barbed wire and all that. It was rather frightening because we didn't know where we were going.

'We were told that it would be a much better camp and this was certainly no lie. By then we had been amalgamated with another group from another transit camp. I am conscious of people on the Isle of Man whom I cannot recall in the first two camps. One man I remember whose mother-tongue was English. He was a Cockney with a broad London accent and he later started English classes on the Isle of Man. There was a much wider spread of people then. There were some Russian Jews who had come to London by the turn of the century and never bothered to become naturalised. God knows how they got classified "B". There was a complete cross-section. Bohemians who took it as it came and blokes like Moishe Bomzer. He was a small man who spoke excellent Yiddish and no other language that we Germans could understand. He was reported to have written to his wife, "Hannah, get yourself interned. You've never had it so good."

'If you can remember seaside resorts anywhere in England with boarding-houses that made up the front, built between 1880 and

1920, it was like that. They were narrow with large rooms on either side of the front door – terraced houses. Several streets were taken over and enclosed in barbed wire, but the football pitch was also included. They allocated fifteen to twenty people to each house. They had been taken over furnished from the landlords. This meant that each room had a double bed.

'So there I was. I had kept company with the boy from Hendon and his father all the time, and in our house there were three other youngsters aged between eighteen and twenty. Each house had a kitchen, and cooking was done in each house separately. When we arrived, we went into the kitchen, which was quite big, and found what looked like bits of leather. It was some time before someone said, "That's dogfish." After Warth Mill anything was all right. At least there was plumbing which worked, and we took turns to wash, shave and what-have-you.

'It was a terribly worrying time for us. By then France had been overrun. By then too we were not treated as prisoners of war any more. The guards knew what we were. The Battle of Britain had begun. We soon had newspapers daily and mail began to arrive. We received parcels, and suitcases with our clothes were sent. Letters from home took twenty-four hours and we ourselves could write to them on special paper. We were therefore in touch with our families. I was not quite aware that the danger was as great as it actually was. We worried about what would happen if the war was lost.

'Physically, we were very well off. There was a canteen where we could buy food; we were sent money. We were better off for butter and eggs than most people because these were sent from Ireland, where they were not rationed, so if we could afford it we could supplement our rations.

'We started organising ourselves on the Isle of Man because by then we knew that internment was here to stay. There were camp doctors and, as we had quite a few Austrians, cafés sprang up. I never ate better cakes anywhere. They could buy the ingredients at the canteen. Lessons were arranged and theatres. There were English lessons, and quite a few people who needed them. We had a very good singer in our ranks, a baritone, and he gave concerts. I was an outdoor bod at that time and was not very interested in lectures. I enjoyed the swimming more. Every day we were marched down under escort to go swimming in the sea. It was fantastic. The relationship with most of the guards was easy-going within a very short period. They organised two houses as youth houses by arrangement with the commandant. People under twenty were supposed to live in them. I did not join them because of my friend's father. He said he was looking after me and the obligation to move to a youth house was removed.

'In July, when "C" category started being hauled in, quite a few of them arrived at Onchan. They thought it grossly unfair that they should be interned; the fact that we should not have been either they could not appreciate. This caused altercations. There was a prison wing, and a young boy in our house got seven days. An advantage of the arrival of the "C" internees meant that we had a large number of people to run the camp; the cooking and cleaning of the houses was done on a rota basis.'

Heinz Kiewe must have arrived in more or less the same 'B' consignment. He revelled in the intellectual life of the camp: 'From the first day, the "Popular University" was arranged and there developed a kind of Chinese news report between the fuchsias in the forecourt of our house. We were some 1500 inhabitants all longing to have something to do and we could give them truly spiritual and visual interests. We had six English-language classes daily, as well as Portuguese, Hebrew, French and Italian. And every afternoon we arranged for a man to speak of his professional life. There were the directors of the Lessing Theatre and the Berlin Volksbühne. There were well-known actors and twelve journalists who later worked on BBC radio propaganda. There were special lessons for the youth group in the youth house. And the rabbis fought in a quite incredible way to conduct Sabbath services. They were infuriated when we arranged a Protestant service one Sunday, and when the local clergyman called at my office and I suggested that he should come every Saturday to speak to us, not on Christianity, but on English history. He was a wonderful man. Soon the Viennese started to do not only cabaret but also music evenings, and it was then that the musicians who later became the Amadeus Quartet began to play together. One wonderful man, a civil servant, wrote a poem every day describing our feelings, and this was put on the wall. At a time when we were not allowed to have newspapers, these were readily read. Soon, the youth house submitted their poetry and we had one German boy who was an absolute poet. One of the most important lectures that we received earlier than *The Times* and the *Daily Telegraph* was a report by an eye-witness of the sinking of the *Arandora Star*. The most famous of all our inmates was Ludwig

Rosenberg, a socialist who gave lectures on the trade unions.

'We had such experts politically that they predicted the news one day before we read it in the newspapers. The British people had our complete sympathy because they did not know what was coming and we did. When they had bombing in London and Manchester, we had our cabaret. The only shot we heard was when a drunk soldier started to shoot outside in terrible weather.

'Looking back it was the anarchist Bilbo who, with his cheek, levelled and raised the inmates behind the barbed wire to one great group of people who contributed to better the position of others. And the Popular University, without any bureaucracy, did its share to that end. Bilbo did not bother with the Popular University, but he did arrange art-exhibitions for all members.

'My father and I shared a room at Onchan. When I was in Kempton Park I wrote on the wall in the washroom, "Here slept Heinz Kiewe, right or wrong. Kind regards from a British prisoner to future prisoners." My father, who was arrested later than I and did not know where I was, was washing his handkerchiefs one day and hanging them by the window when he discovered my writing. He went to the commandant's office and inquired about me. He was sent to Onchan.'

Ramsey gave rise to less enthusiasm. Chaim Rabin writes, 'We had a horrible journey to the Isle of Man. There was a storm and I went on deck because down below people were retching and so on. I did not get sick (I got sick on the way back when it was calm). We were issued with lifebelts. All people could think of doing was stealing lifebelts; they had to do some damage. Afterwards they had the problem of trying to think what they could do with the cork. Could it be used to make ashtrays? Only when they could not think what to do with it, did they regretfully decide not to steal them.

'We got to Ramsey and were put into six or seven hotels. There was barbed wire round the complex but we could walk by the seashore. People actually came and looked at us – like monkeys. We were put into hotel rooms, two, three or four of us, according to the size of the room. Some of them actually had beds. We had palliasses. We cooked our own food in the hotel kitchens. In our house there was a baker who baked rolls every morning. When we arrived, we found the older inmates sitting around with half a pound of butter, eggs and so on – things we had not seen for a long time – because on the Isle of Man there was no rationing. This stopped when we arrived.

'There was not so much intellectual life there as at Huyton, but we were much freer. It did not look like a camp. Once we were even taken to the cinema. The awful thing on the Isle of Man was that the population resented us. We read the newspapers, including the discussions in the House of Keys. They were unhappy because we did not bring in much income. They wanted evacuees. They said, "These people have betrayed their own country. How do you know they'll be loyal to us?" There was much discussion about this.

'I worked quite a lot. I loved washing up and whenever I could I put myself to washing up.'

Already in the middle of June, Rabbi Dr S. Schonfeld, visiting the camps on the Isle of Man on behalf of the Chief Rabbi, could report that arrangements had been made for the provision of kosher food for all orthodox Jewish men and women. The Isle of Man government, which had control of food supplies to the camps, was ordering kosher foodstuffs from Liverpool. In each camp, he said, a few houses had been set apart where orthodox members were accommodated and where kosher kitchens, supervised by representatives of the internees, were maintained. Religious services were held daily by those orthodox groups and on the Sabbath for all Jewish internees.

Both Moses Aberbach and Julius Carlebach had personal experience of such groups at Ramsey. Aberbach arrived there early in June.

'Two of the hotel buildings were reserved for the kosher and orthodox. There were a lot of rabbis there. It is probable that the Isle of Man in the summer of 1940 was the greatest Jewish cultural and religious centre in Europe. It was like a university. There were classes, lectures, discussion-groups from morning till night. Most people had books with them. It was a great centre of learning. A fellow inmate who later became a dentist in Canada wanted to learn Hebrew, and I used to teach him Hebrew on our walks. It went beautifully; he could tell whole stories by heart.

'It could have been a lovely holiday except that France had fallen and the news was terrible. We got suntanned. There were no beds there and we were sleeping on mattresses on the floor. In the kosher houses there was also a shortage of food: not enough bread and potatoes but a lot of herring. I remember being hungry. There were roll-calls every morning and evening but it was very pleasant. There was no work for us. Some people worked in the kitchens; someone who used to have a restaurant was put in charge of the catering and the dining-room and he received the "guests" as if they were his own customers. One felt really at home there.

'The camp commandant distributed leaflets that were left over from the First World War, saying that if we behaved well nothing would happen to us. Then he made a speech, "If you will play the game by me, I will play the game by you." I still remember that good behaviour as a game sounded funny to us.'

Julius Carlebach, seventeen-year-old son of the Chief Rabbi of Hamburg, came to the same spot later: 'I was put into the religious house on *Tisha b'Av* [the Ninth of Av, a Jewish fast-day]. They had no one to read from the *Torah*, but I could and the house was stunned by my performance. I somehow felt that as I had done such a service for them, I was justified in helping myself every night from a box on the mantelpiece in which they put money for charity. I could not think of anyone poorer than I. In the basement there were about a thousand empty lemonade bottles and as my hobby I got myself a broom handle which I used as a spear and smashed every one of the bottles.

'My biggest impression of the Isle of Man camp was of a Reform rabbi there who ate a public breakfast on *Tisha b'Av*. He even ate bacon. I found myself very, very annoyed.'

Eugen Glueckauf remembers the religious house at Douglas: 'There was not much intercourse between the different houses. In one house there was a group of super orthodox Jews. The only thing they would eat was white beans. They spent all day long cleaning them and sorting them out to ensure that there were only sound beans. On one occasion I visited their place and we had a barter, exchanging their meat and butter against our white beans. I thought this was unfair but that was what they wanted. Normally, we used most of our white beans to heat the bath-water. There was a supply of coal and wood, but not enough. These orthodox Jews were very interesting people but they could not talk of anything but *Torah*. The world just did not exist for them.

'I spent these few months in Douglas under holiday-camp conditions, behind barbed wire. We occupied a number of hotels with two people to a room, sleeping in beds. The kitchen was in working order, but there was no one to work it. In my house there was a lecturer in maths called Dr Kemmer; he organised the cooking. He did it rather well. Apart from the fact that the food was not very exciting, there was no hardship. We could go swimming twice a day. When I was not cleaning herrings, I played chess and

HOME OFFICE

# CIVILIAN INTERNEES OF ENEMY NATIONALITY

## Categories of Persons Eligible for Release from Internment

and

## Procedure to be Followed in Applying for Release

*(Revised October, 1940)*

*Presented by the Secretary of State for the Home Department*
*to Parliament by Command of His Majesty*
*October, 1940*

LONDON
PRINTED AND PUBLISHED BY HIS MAJESTY'S STATIONERY OFFICE
To be purchased directly from H.M. STATIONERY OFFICE at the following addresses:
York House, Kingsway, London, W.C.2; 120 George Street, Edinburgh 2;
26 York Street, Manchester 1; 1 St. Andrew's Crescent, Cardiff;
80 Chichester Street, Belfast;
or through any bookseller

1940

Price 1*d.* net

Cmd. 6233

1. The October White Paper pointing the way out

2a.  Marie Neurath

2b.  Ulrich Skaller

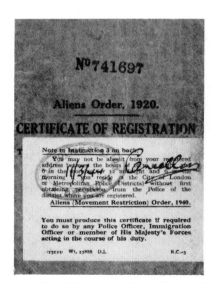

2c.  Ernst Manasse's Alien's Registration Book

3a.   Heinz Kiewe today, with a poster of the Isle of Man 'University'

3b.   May 1940: internees enter Huyton Camp, near Liverpool, an unoccupied housing estate

4b. Stuffing palliasses at Huyton

4a. Huyton

5a.    May 1940: women internees arrive at a London station . . .

5b.    . . . and leave for the Isle of Man

6a. Boarding houses, Douglas, Isle of Man, which formed part of a camp

6b. Internees with a military guard on the Isle of Man

7a.   Onchan, Isle of Man

7b.   Women internees with their landlord and landlady at Port Erin, Isle of Man

Mrs.

Q. Emanuel

1 Wallington Rd.

West Salford 7

Manchester

PAID
POSTAL
15 OC 40

SENDER'S NAME:— Baruch Emanuel
Hutchinson Int. Camp House 10
Douglas Isle of Man

P.C. 66

**OPENED BY**

**CENSOR**

**2778**

8. A letter from Baruch Emanuel

9. A concert programme from an Australian camp

10. Greetings to mother and baby from the men's camp on the Isle of Man

# Sociological Studies

For 7 months and 7 days I have had
the honour of acting as hon. Secretary to the Popular University. This
has given me untold opportunities of
making sociological studies of the
problem I have been working on for 7
years. This problem is the settlement
of thousands of refugees after Hitler's downfall in places where humanity has not yet been superseded by
racial hatred. I had already acquired
considerable experience in refugee
questions: problems of personal
friends, studies at the Kitchener Camp
and other places, and one year of
practical educational work with refugee boys at Ealing Hostel. My experience in the Camp proves the correct-
ness of Leonhard Frank's words: "Man
is good". Friends of mine have warned
me of the danger to compare life in
internment with the realities of normal life. I believe, on the contrary,
that the hot-house atmosphere of a
camp stirs up all human feelings,
evaporates all superficial culture
and shows the true character much
more clearly than under normal conditions. I sincerely believe that our
camp has stood the test. Considering
the strange mixture of Central Euro-
peans, the peculiar habits, ideas and
customs due to different birth, class
and up-bringing, the internees have
behaved extraordinarily well. There
have been no fights nor thefts, and
the worst thing I remember were some
noisy, but quickly forgotten quarrels.
A good deal of friendship, respect
and kindness has developed in our relationships. There have been about
fifty lecturers who, untiringly, have
served the frequently changing community by freely distributing their
knowledge, and have thus given a useful tonic to shattered nerves. Most
of the people who had a say freely
discussed our problems with me. I
gained much experience. I confess, I
learned to understand more of human
nature in these months of internment
with two and a half thousand partly
"de-, ex-, im-, reex- and re-ported
friends than in the past 10 years.

11.   A page from the *Onchan Pioneer*

12b.   A sketch of Australian camp life by Felix Darnbacher

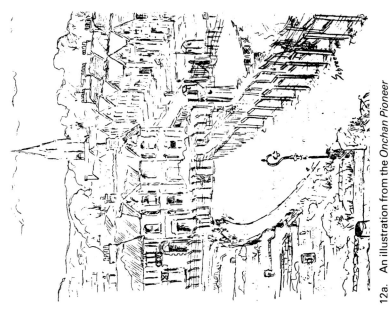

12a.   An illustration from the *Onchan Pioneer*

COMMONWEALTH OF AUSTRALIA.

# Order for Detention of Enemy Alien.

WHEREAS by Regulation 20 of the National Security (Aliens Control) Regulations it is provided that if the Minister or any person authorised by the Minister to act under that regulation is of opinion that it is necessary or expedient in the interests of the public safety, the defence of the Commonwealth or the efficient prosecution of the war to detain any enemy alien he may make an order directing that the enemy alien be detained :

AND WHEREAS the Minister has, pursuant to the provisions of section 17 of the National Security Act, 1939-1940, delegated to me, Captain Albert Richard Heighway, an officer of the Adjutant-General's Branch at Army Headquarters, the powers and functions conferred upon him by Regulation 20 of the National Security (Aliens Control) Regulations insofar as the exercise of those powers is necessary for the purpose of making Orders for the detention in Australia of those persons on board His Majesty's Transport " Dunera," who have been sent from the United Kingdom to Australia for internment in Australia in accordance with arrangements entered into by the Government of the Commonwealth and the Government of the United Kingdom :

AND WHEREAS I am of opinion that it is expedient in the interests of the public safety, the defence of the Commonwealth, or the efficient prosecution of the war that

**Erwin KALLER**                          , being an enemy alien on board His Majesty's Transport " Dunera," who has been sent from the United Kingdom to Australia for internment should be detained.

NOW THEREFORE I do hereby order that the said     **Erwin KALLER**

shall be detained.

Dated this **Sixt h S** day of **September** One thousand nine hundred and forty.

signed. Heighway

*Captain.*

h 2612/40

---

13.   The Australian order

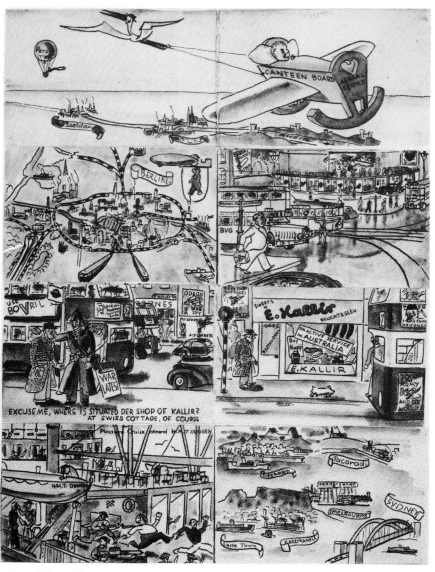

14 and 15.   A farewell card to an internee leaving Australia

16.   The Jewish cemetery on the Isle of Man

bridge. There were quite a number of academically interesting people there. We set up lecture-courses. I too gave a lecture, on "The Analysis of Gases in the Stratosphere", which was one of my researches.'

# 14 The Turn of the Tide

Before the second stage of the general internment policy could come into effect, a marked change in public sentiment occurred. As suddenly as the anti-alien panic had begun in the early spring, so in the first days of July the tide turned. The heightened suspicion waned at the very point when Britain's military situation was at its worst.

Already in June, a modicum of selectivity, even humanity, had begun to tinge internment regulations, a dawning recognition of the fact that internment might actually be hindering the British war-effort. Indiscriminate internment of lads of sixteen, for example, was suspended. Anderson even admitted on 27 June in the House of Commons that arrangements had been made to give special consideration to release from internment in individual cases where it was established that the person concerned was well disposed towards Britain and when the government department concerned claimed that a relaxation of the restrictions would help to further the war-effort. Approximately 340 enemy aliens had been released from internment-camps since 1 September 1939, including children of sixteen and seventeen (allowed to resume their education), nuns (permitted to return to their convents) and technicians needed for special work of national importance.

But perhaps the event which finally tipped the scales of public sympathy towards the enemy aliens was the sinking of the *Arandora Star* on 2 July. This ship, once a Blue Star luxury liner boasting a kosher cuisine, was struck by a torpedo from a German submarine off the west coast of Ireland at six o'clock in the morning on her second day out from Liverpool *en route* for Canada. On board were 473 German and 717 Italian internees. Approximately 146 Germans and 453 Italians were drowned.

Rumours grew and spread like wildfire: the ship had been carrying harmless refugees, as well as genuine Nazis, whom the government was bundling out of the country willy-nilly. The internees had been herded into the bowels of the ship, and when disaster struck had been unable to escape to save their lives. The better-trained, captured German seamen on board had shoved the unpractised refugees aside when fighting for the inadequate life-saving equipment available. And so on. The press contributed its mite, picking up stories purporting to have originated from survivors and publishing them. In *Reynolds News*, for example, H. N. Brailsford wrote, 'It was not a happy ship. Some time before the torpedo struck, the Nazis nailed up a swastika flag in one of the wardrooms, and tried by force to compel the refugees to salute it. A riot broke out, and two hundred men were battened down below. For them there was no escape when the ship sank . . . .'

Gradually and with difficulty some elements of the truth emerged, demonstrating *en route* a degree of administrative muddle difficult to believe even in wartime Britain. Who was responsible for shipping the internees abroad? No one quite knew. After close enquiry it emerged that it was a Committee of the Cabinet presided over by the Lord President of the Council. Who actually had been on board the *Arandora Star*? No one at first was able to state with any degree of certitude – not surprisingly in view of such complications as the exchange of sailing-tickets amongst the internees themselves.

On 9 July the Minister of Shipping gave the first official version when he reported to the House of Commons that the Secretary of State for War had told him that all the Germans on board were Nazi sympathisers. None, he said, had come into Britain as refugees. None had category 'B' or 'C' certificates or were recognised as friendly aliens. But this was immediately challenged. How, asked Graham White, MP for Birkenhead, East, on the following day, could survivors of the *Arandora Star* have told him that there were at least 200 German refugees on board? How, asked John Parker (Romford, Essex), in the same debate, could he have been given the names of two German trade-union leaders, Valentine Witte and Louis Weber, who were definitely known to have gone down with the ship? How could he have been informed that twenty-one Austrian socialists, who had been on board, had arrived safely back in the United Kingdom? These people were hardly 'Nazi sympathisers'.

If the government department concerned (and which government department was concerned?) did not know precisely the names on the passenger list, how much less did the refugee families of interned men know of their whereabouts? In countless homes throughout Britain, people whose loved ones had been taken away and interned and who had not heard from them for days or weeks or months worried about their fate: had they been on the *Arandora Star*? Had they arrived safely in Canada on the *Duchess of York*? Were they being held in camps in Britain? Were they alive or dead? The *Jewish Chronicle* correspondent reported 'harrowing stories' of women who had had their letters returned to them because their husbands had been sent overseas to 'an unknown destination'.

Who actually had perished on the *Arandora Star*? Surely the next-of-kin, at least, should be informed. Osbert Peake gave some indication of the complications involved in answer to a question in the House on 10 July: 'all that the War Office, who have custody of these men, have is a nominal role [*sic*] of the names of those on board. They have to check against that the names of those saved before they can arrive at the names of the missing . . . they transmit those names to the Home Office – I am not sure whether they have been received yet – who transmit them to the refugee organisations because it is only the refugee organisations who will be able to get in touch with the relatives.'

The Home Office had not at that stage received the names of those missing, nor did it receive them for some considerable time.

So great was the general concern that the government established a judicial enquiry. Its report was published in December 1940: all the Germans and Austrians on board the *Arandora Star* had been 'persons who could properly be regarded as coming within category "A"'. The government was vindicated. But that some of those in category 'A' were genuine refugees from Nazi oppression is equally not open to doubt. The process by which the grading took place has already been seen.

And the Italians on board – described by Anthony Eden as 'Fascists' – had never been graded at all. A letter Graham White read out to the Commons on 10 July gives some indication of the type of men involved: 'My mother and I are British born and my sentiments are all with this country. My father, an Italian, came to this country as a young man and fought for the Allies in the last war, when he was badly wounded in the head. He was employed for some years in Folkestone and afterwards in London. He had no political ideas and he did not belong to any association. He lived for his work and home. My parents had never been apart a single day during the whole of their married life. On 11 June he was taken away to be interned. We did not trouble very much as we were under the impression that the tribunal would simply consider special cases.

We received three letters from him, but in his last letter he said he had received no news from us. On hearing of the *Arandora Star* being torpedoed we were rather worried. We found that he was on the *Arandora Star* and posted as missing. Up to the present we have not had any news from the authorities at all. . . . There were 470 Italians missing. Quite a number must have been cruel victims, as in my father's case.'

Other equally horrifying cases came to light later. Colonel Sir A. Lambert-Ward (MP for North-West Kingston-upon-Hull) in October told the House about Gaetino Antonia Pacitto, a naturalised British subject, who was seized by the police at his home in Hull on the night of 10 June. Nothing had been heard of him since. There was also the case, described by Mr Edmund Radford (MP for Rusholme, Manchester), of Clement Fiorini of Manchester, an Italian who had been resident in England for over forty years. He was arrested at his home on 11 June and interned first in Scotland and then at Warth Mill. Thereafter all trace of him appeared to have been lost. In both instances, the Home Secretary regretted that the presumption must be made that they were embarked on the *Arandora Star*. In neither case did their names appear on the list of known survivors.

In the first days of July only first reports and early rumours were available. To many, they were the first intimation of the deportation scheme. The sense of shock was immense.

Sir John Anderson, however, was committed to pursue his general internment policy, despite an interchange in the House of Commons on 4 July: 'Will not the right honourable gentleman agree', asked Sidney Silverman (Nelson and Colne, Lancashire) 'that nearly all the aliens in category "C" were placed there because on investigation it was found that they were themselves the victims of those who are the common enemy?' Sir John Anderson: 'that is the plain truth'.

'In view of the exigencies of the military situation,' he announced on the same day, 'certain further categories of Germans and Austrians now at large are being interned as a measure of precaution. . . . I am taking such steps as are possible to mitigate the difficulties and hardships involved, by exempting from internment certain categories of persons whose position can be distinguished by reason of the value of their services to the national war-effort. . . . The police have standing instructions to give reasonable facilities to an alien to make any necessary arrangements before effecting the internment.'

In fact, before the second stage of internment began, on 4 July, the Home Office had exempted over a dozen groups from general internment. These included people under eighteen who were at school or living in British families, the invalid and infirm, those performing work of national importance, skilled workers in agriculture and forestry, those about to emigrate, those employing at least twelve British workmen, and parents with sons in the British forces. In addition, the police were instructed not to intern in circumstances where to do so would cause 'gross hardship'.

Several German Zionists who had come to England for agricultural training (*hachshara*) to prepare themselves for settlement in Palestine were arrested at this juncture. Among them was Henry Prais, who had arrived in February 1939. At the outbreak of war he tried to join up and was rejected. July 1940 thus found him on *hachshara* in Wales.

'One day in July I was called to the police-station and asked to bring my alien registration book with me. I had never had a German passport; I was born stateless. At the police-station that day, they crossed out the word "stateless" and put in "German". I went back home to *hachshara* and, after thinking about it, I said, "I'm going back tomorrow to complain about the change." So back I went to the police-station the next day, and they said, "How handy you've come. We were just going to pick you up." They drove me back to *hachshara* to collect my things and then back to the police-station. It was then that I met this poor old man who'd been in Britain since before the First World War and had never bothered to get naturalised.

'We were taken to Prees Heath [Shropshire]. This was a tent camp but the weather was still quite pleasant. The internees had the impression that the soldiers had no idea who they were. For the first few days they guarded us with fixed bayonets. After that it percolated through who we were: we were all "C" internees there. The major musicians of the Amadeus Quartet were at Prees Heath.

'During my time there the survivors of the *Arandora Star* came to our camp. Two of them stick out in my memory. One was a member of the German merchant navy married to a Jewish woman, who had had to leave Germany. When the survivors were rescued, they had nothing, but this man had managed to save a pair of nail-scissors. To him, they represented the last vestige of civilised living – and they had been taken away from him by the camp authorities. He was engaged in a life-and-death struggle with the commanding officer to get them back. The commandant was a delightful man. He held "surgery" hours when people could go to him with their problems. This chap went to the commandant about his nail-scissors. The commandant said, "Mr So-and-So, I will see you get them back." And this was repeated at surgery after surgery. Finally, the commandant was thoroughly harrassed and said, "If you knew what fools I am surrounded by in this office: Look, why don't you write me a letter." So the chap went away and wrote a letter: "Dear Captain, I appreciate what fools you are surrounded by in the office . . . ." The captain was absolutely in hysterics, and said, "That was for your private information only. Go back and write another letter." So the chap went back and wrote another letter. He did eventually get his scissors back.

'The other survivor I remember was a man who was a professor in Frankfurt, a non-Jew, who was teaching in Jerusalem and had been studying in England. He got caught while he was in England and had been on the *Arandora Star*.'

Another young Zionist, Henry Berg, also passed through Prees Heath. He had been released from Dachau concentration camp after *hachshara* had produced an exit visa for further training in England, where he arrived in March 1939. In the summer of 1940 he was working on a farm in Berkshire.

'On 4 July 1940 a policeman came to the farm, all friendly. I must have been at work. I was told to pack my things; it would only be a few days – a formality. I took pyjamas and a toothbrush in an attache case. We were taken to Reading. There was nothing to produce any fear. Don't forget, I could always compare it with my previous experience of 10 November. There was nothing to compare with that.

'At Reading, we were just in a drill-hall. There was a constant inflow of people from here, there, and everywhere. No one knew what was happening. I have no bad memories of the whole episode.

'I finished up in Seaton in a Warner's holiday camp. It was one great holiday. We had a good relationship with the guards. There was no aggro' whatsoever. I always involve myself in some activity. I worked in the laundry and in the kitchen. Our accommodation was in huts. I never saw the sea; we weren't allowed anywhere near it. There was lots of barbed wire.

'Next, I was taken to Prees Heath in Shropshire. I remember no hardships. There were various barbed-wire compounds and elevated guards' huts. It had all the appearances of a prisoner-of-war camp. This was the first time I thought, "Well, I'm in for a long time." There was a sense of permanence about it, though we still thought we were going to Palestine.

'Some time during this period an official explained to us that it was not so much a question of getting us out of circulation but of protecting us from people who couldn't differentiate between friendly and unfriendly aliens. Prees Heath was only a transit camp. The selection took place there between those shipped to Canada and the Isle of Man. The question was first raised there too of joining the forces – either the Pioneer Corps or the Jewish Brigade.'

A totally different but also typical internee was Professor Jacobsthal, who wrote a hitherto unpublished description of his experiences immediately after his return from camp.

'On Friday 5 July 1940, in the morning, when I was peacefully writing on Celtic geometric ornament, a knock came at my door in Christ Church College, Oxford, and a plain-clothes police officer entered producing a warrant of arrest. Being an optimist by nature and wrongly believing in English "individualism" I was surprised: there had been a good many other scholars, loosely connected with the University, interned during the last weeks. But I had felt safe: had not the Public Orator in 1937 on the Encaenia mentioned me as "huius Universitatis non inquilinum, sed insitivum" [not a visitor at this university, but rather an adopted son]? I saw the Dean, who tried in vain to obtain from the Chief Constable a respite of six hours, which would have enabled me to shelter my manuscripts and photos properly. I was driven home in the Black Maria, took leave of my wife and fetched my case. On our way back to the police-station we took my neighbour Dr Kosterlitz with his violin, a sympathetic, modest psychotherapist.

'In the police-station my luggage was searched, my razor "temporarily impounded" – they were apparently afraid of suicide or murder (in other places they took more interest in boot-laces). I found the following gentlemen already assembled: Dr Berkenau, neurologist, working in the Warneford Hospital, Oxford; Dr Brink, collaborator on the *Oxford Latin Dictionary*; Dr Forchheimer, head of department in the Austrian Ministry of Labour, then attached to University College; Professor Gruenhut, formerly Professor of Criminal Law in the University of Bonn, then attached to All Souls' College; Professor Jellinek, Professor of Medicine in the University of Vienna, then connected with Queen's College; Dr Meinhart, formerly keeper at the Ethnographical Museum, Berlin, then deputy keeper at the Pitt-Rivers Museum, Oxford; Dr Pfeiffer of Corpus Christi College, formerly Professor of Greek in the University of Munich; Dr Rothfels, formerly Professor of History in the University of Königsberg, then attached to St John's College; Dr Schulz, formerly Professor of Roman Law in the University of Berlin, then attached to Balliol College; Dr Walzer, lecturing in this university on Plato and Aristotle in the Middle Ages; Dr Wellesz, Fellow of Lincoln College, formerly professor in the University of Vienna; Dr Weigert, formerly Professor of Chemistry in the University of Leipzig.

'With only a few of them I had been in contact; most of them were unknown to me. We behaved like recruits on their first day in the barracks. Very soon we made friends and grew into a formation, later on known as the "Oxford group". Professor Beazley came to say goodbye and gave me his *Odyssey* in duodecimo (Oxenii apud Jacobum Parker et Socios, 1899); stamped on the cover "Christ's Hospital"; inside written, "Tu ne cede malis, sed contra audacior ito" [Do not give in to evils, but oppose them more boldly]; he gave me also chocolate and had a pencil and a rubber for me. We had our last normal lunch, served by friendly police-officers. In the afternoon we were driven in a hired Midlands bus to Cowley barracks. There was a detention-room, locked up during the night. We were twelve people, bedded close together on the floor. We had a plain supper in a hall to which we were led by sentries with fixed bayonets. After supper we could walk on a cemented yard twenty-five by thirty-five feet, and look into the country through barbed wire. The sentries, while polishing leather belts and cartridge-cases, talked to us, went to buy cigarettes for us and to post our last messages. Some of us were silent and depressed, others excited and talkative. Professor Jellinek lectured on his experiments on the influence of lightning on metal, illustrated by photos. . . .

'Next day, not too early, we travelled by train to an unknown destination, with an officer and four men in charge of the transport. They were very kind and bought us food, cigarettes and newspapers – the last for many days to come. When, at a small – now, after the removal of name-plates, anonymous – station, we had to change trains and were marching down the platform, we met Thomas Armstrong of Christ Church. He was visibly moved to see his friends, Wellesz and me, as prisoners, one sentry with fixed bayonet in front, and the other behind.

'At 6 p.m. we arrived at Seaton, Devon. . . . We had to march, carrying our rather heavy luggage, from the station, through the village, to the camp. The Seatoners looked at us without sympathy. We stopped at a strong double gate, leading into a huge square with barbed wire round and towers at intervals with sentries and guns on them. The reception was cool; the officers of formal politeness. They impounded my documents, money, torch, penknife, brandy – of which the three last items have disappeared. I now became "R 43938". The behaviour of a corporal when I asked for my confiscated razor was less polite: "You will become very unpopular here if you ask questions." Next morning was a roll-call and then we had to line up for medical examination in case we suffered from venereal disease. There were already about 400 men in the camp. . . . We stayed here for two days.'

# 15 'Some Dominion'

Just as general internment continued despite the changing public mood, so, despite the sinking of the *Arandora Star*, ships continued to leave Liverpool bearing cargoes of internees. On 2 July the *Ettrick* set sail for Canada. On 4 July the *Sobieski* followed in her wake. Leon Feldman was on board.

'One day the order was given and we were taken to Liverpool where convoys were assembled. My "luck" was, I was on the *Sobieski*, a luxury liner, but they had ripped out her innards and made out of her a troop-transport. Obviously, we didn't go on deck at night. We got a lot of air coverage – very good air surveillance. We slept in bunks, six tiers high. The crew was Polish and antisemitic. We didn't know where we were going; we were told we were going overseas. I didn't mind; I was cut off from my parents anyway. I was only worried about my brother. If I got through the war in Canada, I thought, it would be better than that hellhole England. In England we were deprived of any activity: we couldn't work and we couldn't study. We got thirty shillings a week from the Relief Committee, which was too little to live on and too much to die on. Canada and Australia were lands of opportunity. I wanted to survive the war and in England there was fear of invasion. I didn't take a serious attitude to deportation, not like the married or engaged.

'There were three difficulties on the boat. First, there was very little pure water. The sailors pumped in sea-water, purified it and churned it out. We used to take showers from it. Secondly, the crew was very anti-semitic. The basic food was spaghetti. When we asked for it plain and not doused in a non-kosher sauce, they deliberately poured the sauce over it. Lastly, there were prisoners of war on board. Although they were separated from us, it almost came to a boycott. You see, the proceeds from our canteen went to subsidise the prisoners-of-war canteen. Why should we support Nazi prisoners? Any protests didn't help. Even today I have an aversion to spaghetti.'

Martin Ostwald was also on the *Sobieski*: 'We went to Canada on a Polish boat that the Free Poles had brought to England. They put us on the same boat with German prisoners of war. In fact, by and large we were separated, but there was one dormitory where our people and the prisoners were put together. Our people were orthodox Jews and there were immediate difficulties, as they had divided the ship in two: we had the fore and the Germans had the aft. I myself have no unpleasant personal memories of the voyage. There was a convoy, of course, which made us feel fairly safe.'

The experiences of the internees in the Dominions are outside the main scope of this volume and are themselves the subject of books. Here, we shall limit ourselves to brief accounts by Martin Ostwald and Leon Feldman.

Ostwald told me, 'In Canada, we were immediately separated from the prisoners of war. We landed in Quebec City and were taken by train to Trois Rivières. There were already Nazis in this camp (it was by then mid July) and there, on the very first night, there were blood-fights with the Nazis. One of the important things in such circumstances was that there should be organisation, but I can't remember how we elected our first spokesman. However, we made immediate demands for separation and separate kitchens because there were rumours that the Nazis peed into the soup. Certainly the rations were very meagre. The Canadians were flabbergasted to see us, especially the orthodox Jews with their big Talmud folios under their arms and their *payot*, because they had been told by the British that they would be receiving the most dangerous elements.

'Then we were separated from the Nazis and sent to Fredericton, New Brunswick, in the middle of nowhere. We were paid thirty cents a day for work of various kinds; we didn't get currency, only tokens. I was a lumberjack. It was very nice. I once got a job digging post-holes but we could also make army furniture or knit camouflage-nets or work knitting-machines for army socks.

'In our spare time we could have a school. Anyone who knew anything started to lecture. We refused to have any contact with the International Red Cross. The Swiss consul came early on and we refused to have anything to do with him because we were not prisoners of war, and eventually we got special status as refugees. We asked to see representatives of the Canadian Jewish Congress. At first they were afraid of us. And we also got into touch with the Canadian National Council of Refugees. They were marvellous.

These two bodies represented our interests to the best of their ability.'

Feldman elaborates, 'Trois Rivières was a hellhole. It was ghastly – unbearably hot. We were put up in something between a baseball stadium and a fairground. There we were greeted, as we walked in carrying a *Sefer Torah*, by the Horstwessel Song. I distinctly remember the words, "Wenn das Judenblut vom Messer spritzt" [When Jewish blood gushes from the knife]. Finally, they compromised and withdrew the German prisoners of war into another section. This was a stinking place.

'By that time there were constant arguments about whether we should wear prisoner-of-war uniforms. We refused, but the clothes we had lived in continuously had partially disintegrated. And then we started to itch. We thought, "What's going on?" We were constantly cleaning ourselves and taking showers all the time. After two days we found little things at the roots of our hairs. Then we went to the medical orderly. He diagnosed felt lice and said we had picked them up from our mattresses. He ordered us to be shaved completely and said it was lucky we didn't have them in our hair.

'Another problem was that toilets had been installed without doors. We fought tooth and nail about this. Finally, they made half-doors. It was a difficult experience when one was used to privacy.

'When we had arrived in Canada, there had been a mixed regiment – Eskimos, Indians, and all kinds of combinations of races; we could see they were not fighting forces, just for guard duty. One sergeant-major, an American, over six foot tall, a big, husky chap, was Jewish. When they examined our baggage and the guys wanted to take our *tephillim* apart, he said to us in Yiddish, "Take them, and get out."

'Our group was transferred to Fredericton, New Brunswick. It was the first time we had any contact with the Canadian Jewish Congress because by then our protests had become loud: we were not prisoners of war. The local rabbi came to the camp and he helped us with religious supplies, kosher meat, etc. A regular prisoner-of-war camp was set aside for us and we had our own kitchen. There were a lot of cultural activities; a *yeshiva* [a Jewish religious study group] and so on. We always had discussions amongst ourselves and there were a lot of professors and physicians amongst us.

'In Fredericton, when winter came, they took away our civilian clothes and then we had to wear issue. They also insisted that we wrote our letters on prisoner-of-war stationery; the Canadian government said that that was the arrangement with Britain. We debated whether we should make a public demonstration and strike but we were afraid that they would use their guns.

'They forced us all to work and taught us to make fish-nets, which were used for camouflage. It was boring but it did divert the mind and gave us the opportunity to earn the equivalent of a packet of cigarettes and a bar of chocolate a day. They wanted us to work on the Sabbath but we prevailed in this matter. We could also work out of doors. There were a lot of birch-trees and we worked in the forest felling trees. Other teams cut wood with electric saws. It meant that we got outdoors for a couple of hours; one couldn't lounge around all the time.'

# 16 Dark Satanic Mill

One of the most notorious camps was Warth Mill at Bury, Lancashire. A disused cotton-mill, pressed into service early on, it genuinely (and all too sensibly) was purely a transit camp. Peter Katz was amongst the first of its enemy-alien inhabitants.

'After three weeks at Kempton Park we were lined up one morning and told we were being shipped. It was a boiling hot June day and we were kept standing from morning to night. Quite a lot of the elderly fainted; they didn't get much sympathy. In the evening we entrained from Kempton Park station – God knows what time it was; it was dark. The blinds were drawn in the carriages and there was a guard at each end of the train. I did know that we went through London because we used the usual prisoner procedures: one man watches the corridor to see that no one is looking, while another raises the blind to see where we are.

'We were in the train all night, and in the morning found ourselves in Bury, Lancashire. From there we were walked four or five miles – a whole train-load of us, and you can get quite a lot of people on a train. We marched from Bury. That really hurt. We were fighting a war against Hitler and were full of patriotism. If, like me, one came from Germany, one was super-patriotic. And then to be marched like a bloody prisoner of war, with people watching . . . . They didn't jeer because the war hadn't impinged yet. It was the first time I was exposed to the populace and I felt degraded.

'We were marched to Warth Mill, its first occupants. Warth Mill was a disused cotton-mill. It was quite big but it had been condemned in 1937–8 by whatever ministry decides whether a place is fit to work in. It had been left derelict. Some of the machines were still standing. It had a cobbled ground floor and a wooden first floor and a leaking roof. It stank of lubricating oil because all factories then had overhead drives. The smell was horrible and there were no toilets. When we arrived they were finishing off building latrines. It was alongside some canal, which, because it was

97

a hot summer, was practically dry and stank to high heaven. We had camp beds, I think, and army blankets; it would have been unthinkable to sit on the floor. Conditions were so bad that at least three people went on hunger strike and I think that the commandant also protested. He did agree that conditions were appalling and intervened with the War Office. By that time they knew that we were not prisoners of war in the accepted sense and that our interest in winning the war was greater than theirs.

'Seven days later we were moved out. We left early one morning and marched to Bury. It was now mid June.'

By the first week in July, Warth Mill was swarming with interned enemy aliens. Paul Jacobsthal was brought there from Seaton. 'On Monday 8 July we got up at 3 a.m., packed our cases and stumbled through the pitch-dark night with our kit and the blankets to a roll-call in a hall. We tried to remain together but were mixed up with the 400 former occupants of the camp and had to march according to alphabetical order to the station, where a train was waiting for us. We left at about seven in the morning, and travelled northwards. At some station they gave us water; when one of us asked the girl for a second glass, she refused it with very unfriendly words. At six in the evening we arrived at an ugly town which we learned afterwards was Bury. We marched down a long road, Manchester Road, a clue to the part of England where we were. People stared at us with rather hostile looks.

'After twenty minutes we halted in front of a colossal, disgustingly ugly factory showing all symptoms of decay. Behind the wire fences old customers, reduced-looking, low-class refugees, grimaced and shouted at us newcomers – the whole thing a nightmare. We were taken upstairs to a huge hall, about 150 by 120 feet, the ceiling supported by cast-iron columns with Corinthian capitals, along it the remnants of cotton-spinning machinery, transmissions and crankshafts, partly dismounted, heavy pieces dangerously dangling. We had to line up, perspiring, penned together with our luggage; some people fainted. In a corner where through the small windows some light still shone in, an officer and some sergeants were busy making lists and searching men and luggage until nightfall stopped them.

'They finished their job next morning. Five captains, assisted by privates who had the manners and technique of customs officers, were at work: they confiscated books, chocolate, cigarettes, writing paper, drugs; insulin was taken away from a diabetic; doctors had to give up their instruments. I personally managed to keep my *Odyssey* when I showed the captain a certificate with the seal of the University.

'We stumbled through dark staircases and narrow catacomb-like corridors to a hall on the ground floor converted into a kitchen and had porridge and tea in tin vessels. Then we fetched palliasses and blankets and lay down on the floor in the hall upstairs, well guarded by sentries with fixed bayonets. Next morning we learned the name of the camp which now became our home for about a week. Warth Mill – or, as some half-educated internee misspelled it, Wrath Mill, which would have been a far more appropriate name. I have never spent a week in so impressive a place and left it with the feeling of a month's long stay: I shall never forget the smallest detail and I could always find my way through this hellish labyrinth, which had a smack of Piranesi's grandiose *Carceri e Prigioni* [a series of prison etchings by the eighteenth-century Venetian engraver] . . . The building had, to my eyes, the look of the 1870s. . . . The staircases with an open lift-shaft were very narrow, the corridors even narrower and damp. In case a fire was started by an incendiary bomb, not a single man would have escaped; and had a person forced his way into the open air, the space between the walls and the barbed wire would have been far too small. The hygienic accommodation was of a highly objectionable primitiveness: on the premises were – for about 2000 people – sixty WCs, an euphemism, for there were just buckets spreading a terrific stench and no water-flushing system; you could see men of European reputation in an act which is normally not performed in public. One day there was a row: when the internees had been ordered to clean the buckets and the rest, they rightly refused and the job had to be done by other people.'

Ernst Manasse, himself an internee, was one of these 'other' people: 'The toilets for thousands of people were outside under a kind of oblong tent. There were about a hundred toilets with buckets, and volunteers were asked to empty the buckets into big containers. I volunteered for this and we got protective clothing and shower-baths and special food.'

'In dangerous proximity to the cesspool,' Jacobsthal continues, 'so that the doctors among us were very much afraid of infection and epidemics, and pointed that out in a memorandum to the commandant, were huts with water-taps where at one time thirty to forty people could wash, and clean their tin pots. The premises were full of heaps of scrap material and rubbish of every description; sometimes you could see people sitting on an uneven plank supported by two or three bricks they had picked up from the refuse, gloomily staring at the "country" beyond the fence: in the foreground a melancholy stream and a railway; beyond, factories and factories; far away, the faint silhouette of hills of medium height; above, a balloon-barrage. Twice a day for about two hours the main gate was opened and about a hundred at a time let out for a forty minutes' walk on premises opposite, strongly protected by barbed wire and sentries.

'We occupied this hall on the first floor; we were about 400 men, the Seaton group. Other units, accommodated in halls on the ground floor and above us, drew their names from their former camps: the Edinburgh group, the Ascot group, etc. These units were sub-divided into sections, in charge of them were group- and section-leaders, and on top a camp-leader. I shall have to say more of these functionaries. Our group-leader, a metal-worker from Berlin, about thirty years old . . . , mastered the difficult task of commanding this heterogeneous excited crowd and with remarkable impartiality settled the frequent quarrels between socially different groups.

'Already in the train from Seaton to Bury and then in the Mill when waiting for the first formalities, the Oxford group had managed to meet again, enlarged by some adopted youngsters who had attached themselves to us. There was Carsten of Wadham College; Grafe, employed by the Bodleian Library; there were Stein of Brasenose College, Leyer of Magdalen College, Blumenthal from Cambridge, Marcus from Rugby and, the best of all, Gottfried Huelsmann. He was the son of an "Aryan" father and a Jewish mother: he had been brought up in his father's religion, but, under the impression of the Hitler years, decided for the other way. He was proud to have a Jewish passport . . . . Stein, in his Rover uniform, was our "orderly".

'When the Seaton group was divided into sections of twenty-five men, we succeeded in forming one section and in having our palliasses in one row along one of the walls. This was not a matter of class-consciousness – although there was a certain opposition against the highbrow Oxford people – but simply a measure of self-protection, to keep up against very adverse and depressing conditions, to separate ourselves from a fear-inspiring crowd.

'We rose at about seven in the morning and made our beds. Some people got up earlier in order to wash and to shave in the huts before the rush-hour. Some did not wash, and grew beards. I found it more useful to go in the afternoon. Three times a day we marched in groups and sections at varying hours downstairs to the kitchen-hall with our tins and fetched our meals. The cooking was not bad if one remembered that the kitchen was run by amateurs, internees working desperately for sixteen hours or so; it was a very hard job indeed to cook for about 2000 people in a kitchen which was improvised.'

The job had compensations, as Julius Carlebach found out: 'I volunteered for work in the kitchen, which meant that I had access to the two most vital commodities: coffee and meat. It also meant that I had to get up at five in the morning to light the huge Army boilers, field kitchens. From then on, my life in the place was fairly comfortable because I was important. People were polite to me because it could make the difference of an extra cup of coffee. A doctor told me stories about his practice which I thought would help me become a doctor. A writer advised me to keep a diary.'

'Some crooks', Jacobsthal continues, 'always managed to get a second helping with the pretext "for a sick friend". One day 600 rations were missing. It was not easy to carry the filled tins without spilling on the march back through the narrow, dark, slippery corridors, with other men hurrying in the opposite direction. The breakfast consisted of porridge, coffee, two slices of bread with margarine; the lunch of rice or beans and bread; and the supper of coffee or tea, bread with treacle or margarine. On Sunday, we had a very small ration of meat, and occasionally herrings of a very bad quality.

'The canteen sold tinned fruit, chocolate and sweets in small quantities, sometimes an apple or an orange. The difficulty was that our money, taken away from us at Seaton, did not arrive before the last but one day of our stay and we were penniless. I, and some other trustworthy people, gave a collective guarantee to the canteen for £100, thus enabling the rest to improve their meals; it will easily be imagined how much book-keeping was required. The economic system resulting from the peculiar conditions of our life is not without interest. We were without writing-paper, knives, razor-blades and other commodities of primary importance. Some people had been lucky enough to keep this or that. There was no cash; the only tender was cigarettes, and a lively barter set in, everything having its fixed price. Labour was also paid for in cigarettes. The greatest demand was for writing-paper, used for applications: a clever man working in the post-office discovered a large stock of notepaper with the head, "Egyptian Spinners, Hollinwood, Lancs". I still keep some sheets filled with my copy of the first lines of Genesis. Otherwise one had to write on toilet-paper, and this was scarce enough. In our hall there were only tables and benches for about twenty. I mostly had my meals seated on my upright case in front of my bed. After the three meals, breakfast, lunch and supper – there was no tea – one had to go to the huts to clean tins, knife, fork and spoon, as well as it could be done without soda and soap; we made arrangements that one of us did the job in turn for two or three. Once or twice a day was a roll-call in the kitchen-hall; it was difficult to get this undisciplined crowd in order, these individual-ists, unfit for military service, always running about and talking to each other. The atmosphere was so suffocating that not rarely elderly men fainted. Officers and sergeant-majors counted us several times, but there were often too many or too few, and another roll-call had to be held. Occasionally from a raised platform the commandant or other officer made communications on matters of discipline or organisation which one of the German staff translated.

'There was an intense political life – an outlet for suppressed energies; elections every day, candidates addressing the groups, furious debates, malicious attacks – all this very much in the worst German tradition. There was much tension between old age and youth, Jews and Christians, haves and have-nots. Our hall-leader, though brought up in radical circles, had much commonsense and impartiality and we backed him up where we could, but we had to be very careful, for we were unpopular with most people, who were full of social resentment. . . .

'Another distraction and outlet was to make lists and statistics. One day the camp-leader was asked by the commandant to submit at once a list of people in key positions. What was a key position? The camp-leader sent his *aide-de-camp* to consult us: the com-mandant, he said, had tried to find out by 'phone what it was, but had not obtained a clear answer. It was before the publication of the White Paper. When we now made a list for the Seaton group, it turned out that 200–300 people, out of 400, believed themselves to hold such positions. The only thing clear was that none of us did.

'It was too dark to read in our hall; besides the four benches were taken by people playing at cards, and my case was not stable enough to carry my weight except for the short time during meals, so I went to one of the brighter halls on the ground floor, better equipped with tables and benches. There I sat and began to learn Hebrew with Walzer. We had no Bible, but he knew the first chapter of Genesis by heart, and pencilled the words down for me on the notepaper of the bankrupt cotton-mill. I generally sat at a table with a Hebrew poster on it, commonly used by picturesque orthodox Jews with caps, studying Talmud. Once one of them looked interested at my notes and addressed me in modern Hebrew; to his disappointment, I answered in German. Apart from these Jewish scholars, there were only a very few people doing any serious work at all; they had no newspapers and all books had been taken away. They slept or talked endlessly, discussing past or future internment – and release, the great subject. Rumours spread and were willingly given credence: the Germans had invaded Ireland, the French taken Gibraltar, etc.

'One day I paid a visit to Dr Olden in the sick-room, easily the most depressing sight in the camp. The hygienic conditions were revolting. One of the sick told me a rather amusing story. One night a procession enters, at the head a soldier with a candle, then two men with a stretcher and a patient lying on it in apparently grave condition, and, as rear-guard, a soldier with rifle and fixed bayonet. A doctor instructs him to look after the sick man every now and then and to see whether he is still alive. The soldier plants himself by the stretcher holding his rifle and stoops every five minutes, carefully examining his patient. At midnight he goes to fetch a screen, puts it round the stretcher, turns round and says, "Sorry, gentlemen, the man is dead!" and flings himself on a bed. Next morning, a strong voice from behind the screen is heard, "Morning, morning – what is the time?"

'During all these days I picked up many details of people, situations and talk, but, when later on, in the Isle of Man, I went through my notes, I realised that I had seen all through a mist. Those figures moved and talked in an atmosphere of haunted unreality: vision and sound were distorted; the men were hardly themselves; nor was I myself. Most weird were the nights. I was lying between Wellesz and Paul Maas on my poor palliasse through which a sharp break in the floor bored into my ribs or, if I preferred a change, into my shoulder-blades. We did not undress in order to avoid contact of skin with the filthy palliasses and blankets, and to be ready in case of emergency: the searchlights often wandering over the ceiling reminded us of what could happen any night. There being no blackout in the Mill, the lights were put out early. First there was still some talk from bed to bed, and jokes across the hall, songs in German, English and Hebrew; once, from above through the ceiling, a moving performance of a scene from *Carmen*. Then they calmed down and the hall was filled with rhythmical breathing and snoring. It was the real atmosphere of Maxim Gorki's *Nachtasyl* or of emigrants in the between-decks of an American steamer. Soon I got so used to this sort of life that it would have been natural to me to become myself a poor emigrant – and it was hardly a fortnight since I had slept in a bed with good linen, lived a decent life, and had a good meal at home or in Christ Church.

'The day after our arrival we had been told that Warth Mill was only a transitory camp and that we would soon be transferred to another, but it was not till 16 July that we actually left. They sorted out married people between forty and seventy and we had to part with the younger members of our Oxford group – an application that we might remain together had not been granted by the commandant. After the roll-call and return of our blankets and tins we marched down to the station and went by train to Liverpool docks.'

# 17 10 July

If any one date can be said to mark a turning-point in the history of internment it is 10 July. On that date the government held the first major debate on the subject in the House of Commons, and the swing in attitude is immediately apparent. The *Dunera*, with a cargo of some 2542 internees, set sail from Liverpool. And the third stage in general internment began.

Before this third stage, intended to apply to all Germans and Austrians still at liberty in London, local police forces received another letter. 'If internment in your area under stage one or two is not yet complete,' it stated, 'the Secretary of State will be glad if you will instruct your officers that when an arrest is effected the alien should be given a reasonable time for settling his affairs and collecting such belongings as he can be permitted to take with him. In addition, each alien should be asked, when he is brought to the police-station, whether he desires to advance any reasons why he should not be interned. In any cases when the alien makes statements which appear to suggest that he may fall into one of the exempted categories he should be retained in police custody or should be temporarily released while the necessary enquiries are being made.' The exemptions announced for the second stage remained in force. The ice was definitely melting.

Ernst Manasse was arrested under the third stage on 13 July. He had been arrested once before: in Bamberg, after *Kristallnacht*, when he was imprisoned in Dachau. In March 1939 he came to England on the *hechalutz* scheme [agricultural training scheme for settlement in Palestine]. In summer 1940 he and his wife were working on a farm near Charlbury, Oxfordshire.

'In June 1940 I heard from friends in London that internment was taking place. With this, I packed a suitcase so as to be ready for departure. Although I had been classed "C" by a tribunal in Oxford, I was taken into custody by policemen from Woodstock police-station. We were sitting at the breakfast table when two policemen informed me very, very politely to come with them for internment. We had a dog at that time. When I got into the car and we drove off, he ran behind the car. I looked out of the back window and saw him. I said to the policeman, "I must take my dog back." They stopped the car and waited while I took the dog back and locked him up. I could have run away: it was about a quarter of a mile.

'We went to Woodstock police-station and I was the first of the refugees to arrive there. Many more came later. We were not locked up but kept in the guard-room and I told my story about the concentration camp to the police. They wanted to know about it. About midday we were taken by coach to Cowley barracks in the Slade, Oxford, where we were accommodated in the gymnasium. We were served with good meals but we had to sleep on the big mats (used for jumping on) because there were not enough beds. There were, however, plenty of blankets, so we made a pillow from one blanket, and so on.

'Early the next morning we went by coach to a railway-station and travelled south-west, nobody knew where to. All the name-plates in the stations had been dismantled, but some of the refugees recognised some of the towns we passed through. In the late afternoon we arrived at a holiday camp at Seaton in Devon. We were unexpected there and most of us went hungry to bed in a chalet – but there were real beds. Next morning, fresh bread arrived and we had our first meal. We were free to walk around the camp and enjoyed a swim in the pool. We played table-tennis and everything else that was there. We stayed here only one week . . . . '

After a brief sojourn in Warth Mill, Manasse was sent to Scotland: 'After a long train journey we arrived in Greenock, and we went across the water, and then by coach past beautiful lakes, first to Loch Long and then to Strachur on Loch Fyne. We were accommodated in Nissen huts and this was a real holiday for us. When we arrived there it was very dirty because prisoners of war had left there a short time before and they had left everything in a mess. So the first thing we did was to clean up. The food was plentiful and good and the life was easy. We had nothing to do. Some educational classes were established for the English language, medicine (we had so many doctors there) and other scientific subjects, taught by the many Jewish refugee professors. After several weeks we were once more transferred to another camp. Those who wanted to live kosher could go to the Isle of Man. I chose to stay in Scotland and was transferred to Lochgilphead.

'As all the boats had been requisitioned for the evacuation of Dunkirk, we had to go by coach around the lake. It was beautiful, all of it: the landscape, the mountains, the water. And, as it was a hot summer's day, we stopped at a nice bathing-place and those who had trunks put them on and the rest stripped to their pants and we all went in the water. Nobody tried to escape. Even the soldiers guarding us stripped and went in the water. That evening we arrived at Lochgilphead.

'This was also Nissen huts, similar to the previous camp. The food was still good enough but some doctors found out that we needed more fresh green vegetables, which were not obtainable. So it was suggested to the commandant that a party of us go out of the camp to gather dandelions and nettles, and our Austrian chefs understood how to make a very good green vegetable out of them, like spinach. Even in the commandant's office they liked our food so much that we cooked for them as well, for the officers' mess. Occasionally meal-times were delayed because the big kettles did not heat up properly because there was a thick crust of soot coating the outside of them. Volunteers were therefore asked to clean them. I volunteered. There was no protective clothing for this, so I stripped to my bathing trunks and cleaned one of these enormous urns every day. I got a small remuneration and special food (a bigger piece of meat) and certainly a hot shower.

'We had singing classes and we learned Scottish songs – "Loch Lomond", and so on. We gave a concert one evening to which all the soldiers, officers and the commandant were invited. They enjoyed it so much that even the commandant was moved to tears. There were many Christians with us and converted Jews and they tried to convert us to Christianity. There was also a missionary there. The man who initiated the singing-lessons was a teacher of music and we had a male choir.

'One day I had trouble with my teeth. A group of us similarly afflicted, about five or six of us, were gathered together. Transport was arranged and we were taken in an Army truck with an Army driver and a guard with a rifle to the dentist in the village. The driver stayed outside with the truck and we went into the waiting-room with the guard. He left his rifle in the truck. When we came out of the dentist (I had a filling done) the guard had gone. We went out to the truck and found the driver asleep. It was now time to go back to the camp – it was late afternoon by then. When the driver awoke, we drove round the village a few times to see if we could find the guard, but we did not succeed. So we went back to camp without him. It was popularly supposed that he had met up with a girl and spent the afternoon in her bed. We found out later that the rifles were never loaded.

'While I was wandering round the camp one day, I found an empty outbuilding. I explored it and found several big barrels of about two hundredweight each. I sniffed, and smelt, and said, "These are salted herrings." It turned out the commandant knew all about them: they were part of a consignment taken from a captured German cargo-ship. But nobody knew what to do with them. So I washed a few of the herrings and they were delicious but terribly salty and we had to drink gallons of water after eating them. I knew about salt herrings because my mother used to buy them. I said, "These herrings have to be soaked." I found another outhouse where there was a cement floor which sloped down to a drain in the middle. I blocked up the drain with a rubber sheet and filled the room with water and put a lot of herrings into it. Then I took off my shoes, rolled up my trousers and washed the herrings with my feet: I couldn't bend down and wash every herring! Then I drained out the water and filled the room with fresh water and did the same again for the next few days. After that, we had salt herring with baked potatoes a couple of times every week. These were all continental people and they knew about salt herrings. They loved it.

'I used to do some work there. I used to do the washing for my fellow inmates. There was no hot water there in the summer, and no washroom. But I asked permission to do the washing in the bathroom and I used to put all the pants and vests and socks to soak in one bath (I had obtained some sort of washing-powder to make a lather) and all the shirts in another, because I didn't want to mix them up. Then I'd leave them to soak a while. After that, I'd wash them, rubbing them a little bit here and there where necessary. Then I'd rinse them and hang them up to dry in a drying-room where there were a few clothes-lines. I'd open all the doors and windows so that the wind could blow through to dry them. After that, I'd announce, "Your laundry is ready", and all my customers would come and take their own things from the line. There was never any confusion or trouble, even though most of the things were not marked. No one ever took anyone else's clothes. They would just say, "This is mine, this is mine . . . " Then they'd pay me in cigarettes or a penny or something. I was very, very poor at that time.

'We had kippers often in the camp, and our Austrian cook had the idea of boiling the skin of the kippers and using the water to cook the vegetables in. This gave them slightly the taste of smoked beef – but of course, there was no beef there, and we were always looking for it. We had plenty of root vegetables there – turnips and things.'

# 18 Tale of a Tub

And the policy of deportation went on. Hardly had Rudi Guttman been interned than he was on the move again.

'On 10 July 1940, we were put on a train and taken to Liverpool, and in Liverpool we were loaded onto a ship. That's where we got a shock. When we got off the train we were all carrying our suitcases. We started getting kicks in the backside from the soldiers. I got mad at this and one of them shoved his bayonet in my face, so I decided that the better part of valour . . . . We had to turn out our pockets and everything was taken away – fountain pens, etc. People who had rings on had them pulled off. They said, "Yes, you'll get it all back." There was an officer standing there, and one of the older people appealed to him, "What's going on?" The officer said, "Shut up!" '

Felix Darnbacher corroborates Guttman's story: 'We were taken on a train from Huyton to the docks. Up to the moment that the train pulled into the docks, it was very civilised. The British behaved predictably kindly, and the policemen were policemen. From the moment when the doors opened onto the shed at the Liverpool docks, everything changed. It was the same as when the doors opened at Auschwitz. The policeman there said, "Take your gasmasks off"', and helped us cut the string; some people got cut in the process.'

Finally Jakob Felsenstein: 'We were told to pack and to put on our luggage a printed "P" for prisoner. Then we were taken to the *Dunera*. Our luggage was handed in, and the first of us treated roughly but not actually beaten. Later arrivals – and the loading lasted for hours – were handled very roughly. Then the trouble started: our belongings were taken away from us – even our underwear. We were taken below deck to very badly lit accommodation, given hammocks to sleep on. The food was miserable, especially for us who kept kosher.'

Darnbacher continues, 'We were told to take our stuff and go to the wharf, where an enormously big ship was standing. We were told to go up the gang-plank, which was lined with soldiers. The change in atmosphere was immediately perceptible. They said, "Dump your stuff here and go downstairs." People were being kicked in the arse. Down below, they were already being stripped of their watches; that was the moment of truth. We were told to sit down. It was a British troop-ship and we were on a very low deck. There were hooks for hammocks, and mess-tables that could be collapsed. We were told to sit at the tables and put all the stuff from our pockets on them. By then, I had got wise; I hid my knife under the table. They took off my father's wedding ring and he burst out crying. I went up to a soldier and said, "What's going on?" I had a good English accent and father got his wedding-ring back.

'We sat around for a while; there were more and more people coming down. A friend of mine said, "We have to get organised." And so the first organisation started. We had nothing to do but talk, so we chose deck-leaders and boat-leaders and it worked quite well. Then we got under way and went into an enormous squall. Everyone was seasick. It was very overcrowded and we weren't allowed out – the decks were not available. We couldn't open the portholes. People were vomiting, pissing, shitting; they were incapable of getting out of their hammocks. The whole deck was awash with effluence. It also seemed to us that depth-charges were being thrown. It was a very nasty time. It was a good thing that the soldiers were also seasick and therefore left us alone.'

Rudi Guttman elaborates on the 'depth-charges': 'When we left the harbour no one knew where the hell we were going to and rumours were rife. When we got into the Irish Sea it was very choppy and people were sick all over the place; no one was allowed on deck. I went up on a gangway to get a breath of air because the smell down below was ghastly. I was sitting by a pile of suitcases. Then something hit the ship and all the suitcases fell on me. It was a torpedo which did not explode. We had some of the survivors of the *Arandora Star* on our ship; they had been promised that they would not be put on a ship again. They went haywire. I did not know what had happened.'

Jakob Felsenstein did. 'That night we heard a couple of explosions and a short time after a British soldier came to the door and called, "If you heard an explosion, take no notice. We are having artillery practice." There was no artillery practice. The torpedoes had been fired at us. By the grace of God they missed us. It was a stormy night in the Irish Sea. One torpedo grazed the ship; one went past. We would have been completely trapped had the ship been sunk. We never had boat practice. I doubt if there would have been room for all of us in the lifeboats.'

'The first few days', says Rudi Guttman, 'we weren't allowed on deck at all, and with about 2000 people of all ages, and many of them not feeling too good at all, you can imagine what it was like down there. I can still remember the smell.'

Next morning Felix Darnbacher got busy. 'I was not affected by seasickness. I got up, and a couple of other people got up too. We took buckets and started cleaning up – scooping up the effluence from the floor. A sailor gave us mops and squeegees, and from this moment we became the cleaning-party. To be a functionary is to be half-way there. We got soap and flannel cloths which we used to make things with, because we had no clothes . . . .'

And the reason for this deprivation is given by Jacob Felsenstein: 'We saw that the luggage which had been taken away from us had been rifled. I said something about my case being taken away and the officer said, "You have nothing to say in the matter." This was not one of the outrages, but our cases were ripped open and everything was taken away. This happened when we were in the hands of the Pioneer Corps; the Navy behaved correctly. All the outrages were by the Pioneer Corps, including their commander. The instructions given to the soldiers had been quite wrong; we were described as "dangerous aliens". The dominions had undertaken to take "dangerous aliens". This gave the soldiers the right to take all our belongings. That we were anti-Hitler refugees was kept a secret.

'When the soldiers had taken away all they could, they started throwing our luggage overboard, but their own people stopped them by threatening to shoot them. The commander of the U-boat, so he later wrote in his memoirs, saw through his periscope objects floating around the *Dunera*. He thought that people had jumped overboard. He was not willing or able to pick up survivors, but he sent a couple of dinghies to see what it was. They picked up the stuff in the water and found that it contained letters written in German amongst other things. This saved us. The commander radioed to other U-boats in the area to let the *Dunera* pass because they would not want to kill Germans. "Out of the bitter came the sweet": the very act by the Pioneer Corps soldiers who threw our belongings overboard, after they had stolen the maximum they could steal, saved our lives. God's ways can not be fathomed. We don't know why He allowed the *Arandora Star* to sink, but saved us.

'We hid our watches and everything valuable, but one morning I went to the washroom with my watch on. An officer came down the stairs at that moment and simply took it off me. A lot of people had had all their possessions with them (not like me, who had been settled in England for many years): valuables and things like that. They were all pinched. Later on we managed to get together a jumble of underwear which had not been pinched and we put it on exhibition tables under the supervision of trusted internees. Anyone who had lost underwear could claim it, if he could identify it satisfactorily.'

'The only clothes we had were what we were wearing,' adds Rudi Guttman, 'because our suitcases had been taken away. After two days we started a bazaar: all our suitcases had been dumped with all the clothes of 2000 people mixed up. Can you imagine the mess? I didn't find anything of mine. All the suitcases had been forced open and I suppose that the soldiers helped themselves to anything good inside.'

Felsenstein adds a postscript: 'As we passed through Perth, the major who was our commanding officer led an inspection party from Perth on board and showed them through our living-quarters. I happened to be standing near them and overheard their conversation. "What are they doing here?" the Australian asked the major, pointing to our tables of underwear. The major replied, "Oh, the internees have organised their own laundry." Of course, he did not want to say it was the underwear from the rifled luggage.

'The first morning when we had breakfast I saw how depressed people were. I went up to Dr Zimmels, a noted Jewish scholar, and said. "You see how depressed people are, try and give a lecture." He was an extremely modest man; I had to use much persuasion. Eventually he gave a lecture on "Medieval Rabbinical Responsa", which lasted about an hour and was excellent. To this day I find great satisfaction in the thought that I initiated this first lecture on board the *Dunera*. The fact that we only had one suicide during this gruelling journey is largely due to our minds being occupied with lessons, lectures, artistic performances. Because from that one lecture sprang up the "floating university". We had a lot of people with great knowledge and gifts. We could learn on any subject under the sun. This all developed in a matter of days. There was a whole plethora of lectures. In that short time and in those conditions, no other people could have developed such a thing. I took part in Spanish lessons; others learned Ivrit [modern Hebrew].'

Felix Darnbacher echoes this conviction: 'I defy anybody to find a group of people who would so quickly recover from a traumatic experience and organise themselves. There was a blind man on the boat who was immediately used as a walking safe-deposit box. Whatever type of bastard the British Tommies on that boat were, they wouldn't touch a blind man. You see, there were diamond-merchants among us, and they had diamonds with them.

'There were people who had been sailors who made themselves astrolobes and determined where we were. There was a guy called Borkenau who very quickly produced a daily news-sheet from gleanings from the kitchen staff and his own political acumen. He had a theory which we called the *Borkenauischer Rumortheorie*.'

'We did not have much to do', says Rudi Guttman. 'We started playing bridge and held marathon sessions. We had no money so we played for each other's marmalade rations, etc. We had a couple of shows down there, singing, reading and so on. Most of the middle-aged people recited in German – poetry, drama, etc.'

'The religious Jews were quietly sitting in a corner studying the Talmud', Felix Darnbacher continues. But they also organised their own food supplies – as Jakob Felsenstein describes: 'Out of our 2000, about 200 lived kosher and I undertook to go for every main meal with whoever was in the food party to see that our arrangement was working smoothly. We had reached an agreement with those who did not eat kosher to swap: we took more bread and potatoes; they took more meat. And this arrangement did work.

'The food was bad', he continues, 'and the air was stuffy from overcrowding. The light was dim and we were kept under deck for all of the twenty-four hours, except for some twenty minutes when we were allowed on deck. We had to take off our shoes for this because the commanding officer said that the shaking of the ship might be dangerous. So we had to go about in our socks or barefoot. One day, a sergeant broke bottles on the deck so that we should have to walk over broken glass with our bare feet. This shows the spirit of hostility against us.'

Felix Darnbacher corroborates this: 'When we were allowed to walk on deck, there were soldiers with bayonets and rifles all around. We were not allowed to wear shoes because it was bad for the deck. . . .

'We went half way to Canada and then suddenly got orders to go to Australia. We changed course and passed Dakar in Africa at exactly the time the Navy was bombarding a French battleship. Then we put in at Freetown, Sierra Leone, from 18 to 27 July. That was a great thing: there was a blue sky whichever way you looked and a hot sun straight overhead. Boats were coming out with little negro boys offering food. At least one person, if not more, got bitten by mosquitoes and caught malaria.

'Then on 8 August we arrived at Capetown. I saw it through the lavatory window; there was a long queue behind me waiting for a chance to look. At Capetown there was a nasty episode: one man on board was demented and he tried to walk off the boat. They took him down below and we saw him, through a rivet-hole, being beaten up. It was a shattering experience: remember, this was before we heard about Auschwitz. They didn't mistreat me, but they did put me in a cell down below and keep me there for a couple of hours. What happened was that I was busy throughout the voyage making drawings on lavatory paper. I had a green leather windcheater and I hid these drawings in the lining. A soldier, searching me, found them. It was a pity I lost the drawings.'

'When we came to South Africa,' Rudi Guttman says, 'a lot of the soldiers went on shore leave. There was one character on board, a VC from the First World War, a hell of a bastard. He used to lock people up and beat them with a whip. I was locked up but not beaten. A few people got beaten up by soldiers, particularly one boy who had only one arm. I do not know why, but they always picked on him. One guy jumped overboard. They used to have searches down below when we were up on deck. I do not even know what they were looking for. There were one or two reasonable people, generally members of the ship's crew. We appealed to the captain and the commanding officer of the troops, but I personally was not active in the protest movement. However, I knew that all sorts of petitions were handed in. But things did not improve. After Capetown, in fact, things got a bit rough because the soldiers were drunk. While there, we were not allowed on deck.

'As we got into hotter parts things got quite uncomfortable down there. But I never got depressed. We lived in shorts; they were the only thing I had. I had had long trousers but I had cut them down.'

On the *Dunera*, one internee records, 'two people succumbed. One was killed in a fight. He was supposed to be a professional boxer and a bully. He challenged someone who was afraid of him to a fight. He had a weak heart and died. There was another chap who could not be buried because he jumped overboard. The story was that he had some documents to enter one of the more obnoxious states in South America. They had expired and he did too.

'In the ship there was a mixture of all sorts of people: Communists, people who had been in concentration camps, orthodox people with black hats and long hair and who had a bit of a supply problem. The soldiers pinched what they could and the people themselves were not altogether honest. After a few weeks we had vigilantes of our own to see that things were not stolen.'

# 19 The Swing Back

On 10 July German 'planes carried out the first large-scale daylight raid of the war on Britain. It ushered in the series of such attacks which came to be known as the Battle of Britain.

At half-past five that afternoon, the House of Commons embarked on its first large-scale debate on the question of the refugees. Members spent six long hours discussing the rights and wrongs of government internment policy.

The mere fact that such a debate was held at such a time is itself indicative of the changed attitude towards internment and the strength of the feelings aroused by previous policy. There was, it would appear, a growing recognition that injustices had occurred, that skilled manpower was being wasted, that administrative muddle had caused unnecessary hardship and that wrong criteria had been employed.

That general internment was essential for national security was argued only by a few lone voices. 'I know that I am speaking against the sympathy of the majority of the House', admitted Mrs Mavis Tate, MP for Frome, Somerset, questioning whether 'so-called victims of Nazi and Fascist aggression' had not in the past been useful tools in other countries. 'I took up the view', said Maurice Petherick (Penryn and Falmouth, Cornwall), 'that all enemy aliens should at once be interned in concentration camps from the moment war broke out.' 'Why should we trouble if one or two, or a thousand, suspects are interned,' thundered David Logan (Scotland, Liverpool), 'if this land of ours is safe?' Sir Edward Grigg, Joint Under Secretary of State for War, tended to agree with him.

That general internment was positively damaging the nation's war-effort was a view more frequently expressed – and not only by the acknowledged friends of the refugees, Major Cazalet and Eleanor Rathbone, who opened the debate. On an ideological plane, it was first and foremost harmful to Britain's reputation, in the eyes of the world, as a haven for the persecuted and oppressed. It was supplying the German propaganda machine with valuable ammunition if it could claim that Britain was pursuing the Nazi policy of interning Jews. Most important was a point raised by Sidney Silverman: 'Our main hope of bringing this war to a successful issue', he reasoned, 'depends on convincing those countries which are still neutral that we realise that this is a war of ideas and that we are fighting for the right idea. It depends also . . . on winning and retaining support for our cause inside the enemy countries themselves, some portion of whose population . . . are as much anti-Nazi as we are.' It should be borne in mind that America at this juncture was still neutral.

The concept of the war as a war of ideas, crucial to understanding the problem of the refugees, was spelt out several times during the course of the debate. Osbert Peake put it succinctly: 'labels of nationality in Europe in the last twenty years have meant very little. They are no guide . . . to the sympathies of the individual or to his reliability.' That repetition of this definition was necessary, is shown, for example, by Logan's comment in relation to the disaster of the *Arandora Star*: 'What sympathy has been extended to the refugee boat by the country which torpedoed it? If that country can do this to its own people, why should we waste time with the problems of aliens instead of dealing with the protection of our own land?'

On a practical level, general internment of enemy aliens was positively detrimental to the war-effort, in that it was immobilising a source of invaluable labour-power. Skilled scientists and engineers, medical men and writers were languishing behind barbed wire in idleness when they could – and indeed wanted – to use their abilities to defeat Nazism. Able-bodied men were lounging in boredom in the camps when they could – and wanted to – fight on the battlefields or till the soil. Business-men had had to close down factories, throwing British workmen out of jobs and cutting national production. And the majority of these men had passed through at least one tribunal and been graded 'C', as refugees from Nazi oppression.

These were the major themes aired, but the sense of muddle running through the execution of internment policy, attributed partly to the apportionment of responsibility between two ministries (the War Office and the Home Office), partly to the scope left for the police to exercise their discretion, was never far from the surface –

and not only in relation to the *Arandora Star*. Individual instances of mismanagement abounded. Josiah Wedgwood told of an old officer of the Austrian Army who had struggled for two years to get a visa for New Zealand for himself, his wife and his child. At last the visa arrived and they were due to sail on 4 July. On 1 July he was arrested. Neither the War Office nor the Home Office could find him in time for him to catch the boat. He was mislaid . . . . Philip Noel-Baker (MP for Derby) read out a letter he had received from another internee: 'Age 53: refugee from Nazi oppression: "C" class: arrested in the streets of Leipzig during November pogrom; three months in Nazi concentration camp where he contracted diabetes. Now living on daily insulin. Only child in English sanatorium with chest disease; offer to serve Britain three times refused. Has this morning been detained by CID men for immediate internment as enemy alien. Fainted: carried away semi-conscious. Here's to victory.'

But it was left to Eleanor Rathbone to tell the most tragic tale. It concerned a German professor of chemistry, sixty-two years old, an international authority on dyestuffs. In Germany he was in a concentration camp. When he was released he came to Britain, where he was given a research grant. For the past year he had been employed by a company where he had been developing a process for utilising sisal waste particularly for use in submarines. His firm applied to the Home Office for exemption. At the beginning of July the police called at his flat. He showed them the application to the Home Office and asked them to wait until it had been investigated. They refused and told him they would come back shortly. He warned them he could not endure another internment. They came back two hours later to find him dead. He had taken a quick poison.

The arguments and all the tales of tragedy did not bring about an immediate reversal of the policy of general internment. Arrests continued throughout July at a rate of 150 a day in London and Manchester, according to the *Daily Telegraph*. The *Jewish Chronicle* regretfully reported that the exemptions that Peake had promised were not always being observed by the police. By the middle of the month some 12,500 men and 3800 women of German and Austrian nationality were interned in Britain, and some 7350 male civilian internees had been sent overseas.

The arrests in the second half of July were concentrated in London. Amongst the victims was Martin Freud, son of the psychoanalyst. 'If the famous Freud had not been wise enough to die,' commented the *Daily Mail*, 'he would by now have been interned. Lucky for Goethe and Schiller and Heine that they are all dead too.'

A police round-up in the East End of London caused something of a stir at this point. The total population of College Buildings, Wentworth Street, signed a petition for the release of three local traders who had been taken away, it was claimed, at less than an hour's notice. The interned men had conducted their businesses across the road from the entrance to College Buildings for thirty to forty years.

Peake said during the course of the 10 July debate, 'At one time the feeling in the country and in this House was entirely in favour of the refugees. That feeling changed in the early days of May. Today it is swinging back in the other direction.'

Large sections of the press now proved him true. A letter in *The Times*, for example, signed by the Master of Balliol and five prominent University figures asked that the process of reclassification be carried out with the least possible delay and 'in the meantime, it is important that we should administer our camps with common sense and with such humanity as is possible in war-time, remembering that the vast majority of the human beings they house are not our enemies but our friends'.

Hannen Swaffer in the *Daily Herald* exposed the case of the Treforest Trading Estate, started with government money in a distressed area of South Wales. Eighteen Germans and Austrians had started factories here, many of them introducing new industries to Britain, employing 1035 previously workless Welshmen, after teaching them new skills. Sixteen directors or keyworkers had been interned and the rest had been ordered to leave the district because it was declared a protected area. And yet each employer before he began had been vetted by six government departments and all the trade organisations in the various industries.

H. G. Wells in *Reynolds News* began a series of articles attributing the policy of general internment to treachery. 'This is not a case of administrative stupidity . . . it is a case of "doing Goebbels's work", of enemy activity entrenched in our midst. . . . The hard necessity of our present situation is to identify, punish and repudiate that nest of traitors immediately . . . .' The *Jewish Chronicle* favoured this theory, hinting at 'a spirit of ugly treachery in certain influential quarters, treachery which rejoices as much in inflicting misery upon Hitler's refugee enemies as in damaging the interests of this country'.

'SHAME', was the headline in the *Evening Standard* on 23 July. Eye-catching italics informed readers that *'The good repute which we have gained over centuries for humanity and an inveterate love of freedom is being wantonly and shamelessly besmirched.*

'As Hitlerism swept across Europe, a great company of peoples were driven along the roads of Germany, Austria, Czechoslovakia, Belgium, Holland and France. They were the weak whose only crime was their race or the brave whose only crime was their defiance. Some stepped on our shores and drew a deep breath of freedom. They were ready to serve and work and fight for England, for England's cause they believed was the cause of free men the world over.

'What have we done with these, our friends? . . . It is folly. . . . It is worse than folly. It is sabotage against our war-effort. It is a damnable crime against the good name of England . . . .'

On the same day as this article appeared, Sir John Anderson made a statement announcing the government's measures to rectify the situation. There was no question at the present time, he said, of reverting to a position in which the internment of men of enemy nationality would be the exception rather than the rule. But it was clear that further examination would be likely to disclose in a number of cases circumstances justifying the release of individuals interned in the pursuance of the general policy.

To that end, the instructions for the exemption of certain categories of 'C' grade aliens issued for the 4 July round of internments would be given retrospective effect. Steps would be taken for the release of men who had been interned before the instructions came into force but who would have been exempt under their terms.

There had also been cases of mistakes in interpreting the instructions, Sir John admitted. 'These mistakes must be rectified with the least possible delay . . . .'

To help him deal with this problem of the control of enemy aliens, he had decided to appoint a small advisory committee. It would, first, keep under review the application of the principles laid down for the internment of enemy aliens and make suggestions regarding it to the Home Secretary. Secondly, it would advise him on any proposals for modifying internment policy he might refer to it. Lastly, it would examine and make recommendations on individual cases, or groups of cases, he might refer to it. This committee came to be known, by the name of its chairman, as the Asquith Committee.

In addition Sir John announced that he had decided to transfer to the Home Office responsibility for the welfare of the internees. 'When it had been necessary to make rapid arrangements at short notice for the custody of a large number of persons, it was essential to make use of the military organisation for this purpose. No other organisation could have coped.' But, as Sir Edward Grigg had said on 10 July, it should not be the business of the Army to look after civilian internees. In future, the Home Office would be responsible for managing the thirteen camps, although the War Office would continue to bear the responsibility of providing the necessary camps and the service personnel to guard them.

An advisory council was also to be appointed, attached to the Refugee Department of the Foreign Office, and concerned with the many nationalities of alien then in Britain. Its chairman was to be Lord Lytton. Its functions would be to suggest measures to maintain the morale of these aliens so as to bind them more closely to the common cause; to review and, if necessary, to suggest measures for the co-ordination of the work of the various refugee committees for that purpose; to maintain contact with the various government departments having responsibilities in connection with refugees and with foreign governments or national committees in Britain; to advise and assist the Home Office in its arrangements for the welfare of enemy aliens in internment-camps; and to study and make recommendations upon the problem of finding occupations for them.

'It is the desire of the government', said Sir John, 'that everything possible shall be done to alleviate their position, and in particular to ensure that internment shall not involve conditions of enforced idleness.'

He might have expected that the statement would be greeted with cheers of approbation. If so, he must have been disappointed.

The statement, said Josiah Wedgwood, missed the whole point. Instead of categories to be left out of unjust imprisonment, there should be categories to be retained in imprisonment.

So strong did feelings run that the Speaker on this occasion and on 25 July had forcibly to call a halt to questions.

Sadly, on the very eve of surrendering control of the camps to the Home Office, the War Office dropped another blot on the

'bespattered page' of internment history. Forced for some unspeci-
fied reason to vacate Kempton Park camp in haste, it transferred
some 700 internees with an average age of over fifty to Sutton Park,
Sutton Coldfield, which was inadequately, if at all, prepared for
their reception. It was a canvas camp with, said Eleanor Rathbone,
not a bed, not a palliasse, not a chair. Sleeping seven to a tent, the
internees lay on the bare ground. This camp, in its turn, was vacated
in a hurry, three weeks later.

On 31 July a government White Paper announced that the
Secretary of State was prepared to consider the question of releasing
from internment 'C' grade Germans and Austrians falling within
one of eighteen categories – with the proviso that release could be
refused on security grounds. The categories involved were as
follows: (1) persons under sixteen and over seventy; (2) those under
eighteen who, at the time of internment, were resident with British
families or in educational establishments; (3) the invalid or infirm;
(4) people who, when interned, held a permit for their employment
issued by the Aliens War Service Department, or (5) had permission
from the Secretary of State or the local Chief Constable to remain in
an aliens protected area; (6) those who occupied key positions in
industries engaged in work of national importance; (7) skilled
workers in agriculture, commercial food-growing or forestry;
(8) scientists, research workers and persons of academic distinction
for whom work of national importance in their special fields was
available; (9) doctors of medicine and dentists who had been authorised by the Secretary of State to study in Britain for British
degrees and who were pursuing their studies to that end, or (10) to
exercise their professions in Britain; (11) persons who, having served
in His Majesty's Forces (including the Auxiliary Military Pioneer
Corps), had been discharged on grounds not reflecting on their
loyalty to the country or their personal character; (12) internees
who were accepted for enlistment in the Pioneer Corps; (13) persons
engaged in refugee organisations which were still functioning;
(14) people who were employers of at least twelve British employees in
works or factories engaged in work certified by a government
department to be of value to the community, if it could be shown
that, unless the alien were released, the business would have to be
closed down and the British employees discharged; (15) persons
having a British-born or naturalised son serving in the British armed
services; (16) ministers of religion holding a spiritual charge, except
ministers of the German church; (17) persons about to embark for

emigration overseas; (18) special cases of extreme hardship.

The document also mentioned the possibility of further categories being added as the result of the review which the Secretary of State had asked the Advisory Council to undertake.

At the end of July arrests of enemy aliens in London and Manchester were temporarily suspended. Around this time too (1 August) it was announced that the Home Secretary did not propose that any more civilian internees should be sent overseas unless they had either volunteered to go or arrangements had been made for them to be accompanied or followed by their wives and children.

At this, the turning-point in internment history, 27,200 men and women had been interned, of whom 7350 were in the Dominions.

# 20 The Isle of Men (II)

On 29 August 1940 the young Baruch Emanuel wrote to his Aunt Rosi in Manchester from Hutchinson camp on the Isle of Man, 'I was, as you may already know, interned on 12 July and almost immediately taken with two other young men from my *Beit Chalutz* [hostel for agricultural "pioneers"] to Douglas, Isle of Man. The camp here is quite wonderful. We have a meadow where we can stay out in fine weather. Every day there is either a walk or we go swimming. We are three minutes from the sea here and always pass Central camp when we bathe. During the day I work in the shoemakers' workshop, where I am very well treated. . . . please give Uncle Isskar my good wishes. He should be as happy in his internment-camp as I am here.'

Not all of the large number of 'C' grade men brought to Hutchinson camp in mid July were so simply satisfied. The reactions of Paul Jacobsthal were, perhaps predictably, more complex.

'We went on board the *Tynwald of Douglas*, a queer old vessel of Dunkirk fame, quite unfit for the accommodation of 700 men. It rained and we had to crowd downstairs on the floor like cattle or slaves. The food from Warth Mill had been just enough for lunch; nothing was to be had on board. There was no restaurant, and a poor canteen sold only poisonous lemonade and an insufficient quantity of biscuits. I lived on a piece of chocolate for twenty-four hours and was lucky enough to get half a bottle of tea, through bribery. An old, sick man died of exhaustion. We had gone on board at three in the afternoon and we were anchored in the Mersey until six in the morning. I thought of the men who had travelled in the *Tynwald* from Dunkirk and I did not complain as so many others did. But I also thought that they had done it for a good cause and that I was a victim of a very stupid measure of no avail to the country. At six in the evening we weighed anchor and after a pleasant crossing of four to five hours we arrived at Douglas. They counted us four times and we marched along the quay, flanked with big, now empty, hotels, to the "acropolis" of the place.

'There were already about 500 men arrived before us at Hutchinson camp. We had to line up in front of the houses which were not yet occupied, in groups of about twenty men. When we entered the house assigned to us, it turned out that there were two distinct groups, one consisting of academic people, the other of Jewish business-men, unknown to each other and looking at each other with hatred, all very tired: the atmosphere was dangerously electric. One of the second group . . . got into a rage and shouted through the window for a doctor. I realised that something had to be done to prevent an explosion and I exercised my authority and gift as a mediator, bullying and soothing. . . . I placed them at the tables in the room on the ground floor and patiently made a scheme for accommodating them: there were seven rooms of which most had double beds for two people, but there were mattresses for those who preferred to sleep on the floor. The problem was solved almost to general satisfaction. A small room in the attic, with top-light only and very small, was given to Professor Weigert because he was the worst snorer of us all. I was to live in a small back room with Wellesz and Pariser, the latter lying on a mattress and his private pneumatic sleeping-bag. This being done, I fell back into privacy and proposed Dr Loening as house-father; he was unanimously elected. Afterwards, he tried to resign office every week for various reasons, but I always successfully persuaded him to carry on.

'House 24 was, like the others, a boarding-house with nine rooms of small sizes, one bathroom and one WC; in normal times, before being commandeered for internment purposes, lodging, I suppose, ten people of a class able to afford thirty shillings for full board. We often thought that it would have been much worse to have a voluntary holiday in this place. The furniture was poorer than in most of the other houses and we had not even chairs in the bedrooms, and I often read and wrote sitting on my bed with very little light shining through the small window, covered with a poisonous blue for ARP purposes. The beds were in a bad state of repair; people under fifty-five had two blankets and over fifty-five three; there was no linen. We had no electric light in the bedrooms and it took weeks before, through theft and bribery, we got hold of three bulbs for kitchen, staircase and common-room. The last, fifteen feet by fifteen feet, had two tables, far too small for eighteen men. Also many other requisites in the kitchen and bedroom were missing, but we had Richard Cohn, a man with an inventive mind and a sound training in occupied countries in 1914–18, who searched for scraps in basements, stole wood, nails and screws and made shelves, commodes or lampshades out of nothing. The worst thing was that the blackout regulations in the camp had to be very strict: the commandant was always having trouble with the Manx, who talked of signals given by the internees; and, having no curtains, we had to sit in complete darkness after blackout time.

'The original scheme that the house be cleaned and kept in order by all the inmates in turn did not work, because most of us had hardly ever handled those tools before, and after some days the practice was adopted that every one of us made his bed and swept his bedroom, but that bathroom, staircase, common-room and kitchen, washing of crockery and so on, were done by people more familiar with this sort of job and glad to have twelve shillings a week for their cigarettes. The house had to do the cooking and received the raw materials from the store; five of us in turn were the "bin-carriers": we had to line up after lunch at the camp-gate and fetch the stuff from the store. The empty vessels had to be returned in a clean state the next morning before ten. The food was quite sufficient in quantity, but somewhat monotonous and poor in quality, especially meat, fish and margarine. There was a surplus of carbohydrates; we never had eggs and rarely vegetables. There was also a certain lack of fat, but our clever cooks got margarine from the kosher houses, giving them beans, of which we had too many, in return. In September, when younger people went on farm work in the isle, it was possible to buy butter in great quantities – butter was not rationed here – but soon crooks started a business, paying the boys 1s 8d a pound and selling it for 2s 8d. This went on for a fortnight until the commandant very rightly stopped the farm work and put some of the profiteers in prison.'

Erich Mark, who went to the Isle of Man at the same time, adds a comment on the food: 'It tended to be better than at Lingfield, but I remember the occasional lapse, and this was vividly illustrated by a consignment of gone-off kippers which we hung on to the barbed wire in the main street until putrefaction gave them a fine glow in the dark. Our staple cabbage was said to contain a goodly dose of bromide to keep our male feelings under control.'

Jacobsthal continues, 'The canteen, for reasons unknown to us, was always ill-assorted, worse than that at Warth Mill. Mostly one could only buy tobacco, stationery and some more or less useless articles, sometimes, but too rarely, an apple or an orange. Even if the canteen had been better, the lack of cash would have been a serious obstacle. Most people had money enough in their accounts with the camp bank, but no man was allowed to draw more than ten shillings a week; this was, the commandant thought, a measure of social justice. "In this camp, the Oxford professor will not be treated any better than the scavenger among you" – to quote his words. Ten shillings was not enough for paying for laundry, repairs to shoes and clothing, and buying tobacco and some extra food. It soon occurred to us that we could get cash from people who were released, when they were paid their balance from the bank; we would give them a cheque in return. Some people got parcels from home, Pariser every day. They arrived without delay and were not censored in Liverpool like the letters. There was a special parcel department in the commandant's office where captains for at least four hours a day opened the parcels with the utmost patience and cheerfully chatted in English or German to the addressees, while unwrapping the tins, boxes or clothes. I have never understood why this boring job was done by highly qualified officers and not by picked privates or sergeant-majors, as would have been the case in other countries.

'The transformation of the raw stuff into edible food was no easy matter. Of the two cooks which we employed during the first weeks, Herr Gruenspan, an amiable Austrian, was not at all bad, but without imagination; the other, Finkler, an Austrian forester who had had to leave his country because he was a monarchist, was a crank and there were always rows between him and the "Jews" in the house. He was replaced by a *chef de métier*, Herr Hirschfeld, once a civil servant in Hamburg, who before his emigration had taken a course in cooking. He had technique and fancy and a good education. But the best cook in the camp was Dr H. Weissenborn, formerly professor at the School for Graphic Arts in Leipzig.'

Jacobsthal was very conscious of the division between the academics and the business-men in No. 24. The business-men 'had their bridge parties, read their cheap books, had their sort of talk, but did not mind if our habits and pleasures were different. I succeeded even in getting them to some of our lectures, which were of interest to them, and, when, in the last week of my stay, I lectured myself, it was a matter of course that the whole crew of No. 24 attended and, I think, enjoyed and understood what I was talking about.

'I have – an inheritance from my father and mother – never been class-conscious. It was an honour and reward to me that they trusted me and let me see into their private, mostly sad, affairs, and sought my advice. These months were a great lesson to me. My wife and I had left Germany in time and been spared the horrors of real and cruel persecution, of which we knew only by hearsay or from *The Times*. We had been living in Oxford and with our English friends and knew little of refugees and their problems. Now I was living with men who had suffered terribly. They spoke rarely, but the more impressively, of their ordeals in concentration camps. Once far better off than I, they had lost everything and now with dignity led a life of privation in exile, eager to emigrate to America and to build up, if they could, a new existence.

'House 24 was one of about forty boarding-houses requisitioned for the internment-camp, forming two rows round Hutchinson Square (about 300 by 150 feet), these built of yellow brick in a style of timeless, undatable ugliness, and there was a third parallel row with more pretentious grey houses dating from the eighties or so. Each house had a small front garden with hortensias and some with a palm tree. The backyards were as ugly as in Manchester or Liverpool. The whole was enclosed by a double barbed-wire fence . Outside the camp proper were the commandant's offices; people who had business there had to have a pass and were let out by two sentries who had key positions at the double gate.

'The square was planted with flowers and shrubs and was kept in order by internee gardeners. It sloped slightly towards the sea. From the top, one overlooked part of the bay with the islet of Conister, with a tower of refuge and a lighthouse and a hill with some fortress-like building on top. From the upstairs rooms one could see the distant hills inland. During July and August, as long as the weather was sunny and rainless, the lower part of the lawn served for gymnastics, lectures, Jewish services, even concerts, or it was used as a putting-green.

'Hutchinson internment-camp was run on the same lines as all other camps, probably on a central order from the Home Office: self-administration of the internees under the control of the military authorities. A wise system, developed in the colonies where the natives were clever enough to look after themselves, and these "natives" were very clever indeed. Each house had a house-father, elected by ballot for a limited period. They met every day and discussed affairs of public, common interest. Three or four of them formed a special committee with a lawyer, a doctor and a rabbi(!) as advisers. On top, appointed by the commandant and responsible to him, a camp-father. No internee was allowed to approach the military authorities directly, neither to write nor to speak to them. Everything went through the house-fathers and the camp-father. Post-office, camp bank, canteen and, to some extent, the hospital were run by internees, and some of them were also working in the commandant's office and the parcel and intelligence department.'

Erich Mark was one of these: 'I volunteered for work and was assigned to the office, located just outside the fence in similar sorts of houses to our living-quarters. . . . My office-work consisted of filing documents, listing possessions which had been taken from us on arrival at our first camps and eventually, as life settled down to some normality, returned. There were sickness reports, roll-call lists and so on, and, in between, chatting to the guards' own office personnel. Meals were now arranged by houses or groups thereof, and the office was only open in the morning, so that afternoons were leisure-time.'

Jacobsthal did not whole-heartedly approve of this activity: 'It would be unfair to deny that most of these people worked very hard and usefully, for they had all the virtues of the German race, efficiency and the gift of organisation. Especially a man, working in the release department, did much to speed matters up, and many people would have come out a day or two later if he had not patiently and selflessly spent his nights filling in and preparing forms which the officers had to sign. But I have always loathed subalterns, giving themselves airs and trying to fraternise with their superiors. And to wait an hour in the intelligence officer's antechamber, to be asked by one of these German creatures what my business was, and to show him my letter first for approval before I was let in was exasperating, and I was sometimes on the point of tearing a letter up rather than undergoing this humiliation.

'The English officers were well chosen and some of them spoke German excellently. Here again the experience of a nation with colonial tradition was visible: one of the intelligence officers had worked before in Bloomsbury House. The most important figure was the sergeant-major, a stout, jovial man, always gesticulating with a beautiful brass baton, a present from his Indian natives. My contact with the officers was confined to the very few occasions when I had to call for a parcel or to submit for censorship an extra letter to the intelligence officer. I had also a five minutes talk with the commandant when I was released. They were very polite and, it seemed to me, quite aware of the absurdity of my internment, though none of us spoke of it. Collaboration between the military authorities and the internees worked smoothly and satisfactorily. But there was one delicate problem. The very sincere and humane commandant had the ideal of a "happy family" – the words are his. This meant that he came to the concerts. Officers even attended performances of the highly objectionable *Cabaret Stacheldraht* [Barbed-Wire Cabaret; more of this later]. He had a hall built for meetings, prepared a scheme for a library and the artists were asked to decorate offices with paintings. But I found that men of higher moral standard held the view "I am either an internee or a free artist", or "You cannot have your cake and eat it", and were afraid that one day some stupid and servile ex-internee would write a letter to the editor of *The Times* with a vivid and edifying picture of the "happiness" in Hutchinson camp. I personally was not in a position to take a stand on this problem, but I always avoided attending any performance where I was likely to meet officers.

'The skeleton of our daily existence looked like this: we rose at 7.00–7.30; had breakfast at 8.00; before or, as the days became shorter, after this, there was roll-call. We lined up in front of the house, or, if it rained, indoors. The house-father reported to the two or three officers and the sergeant-major counting us: "House 24, eighteen men, one in bed" (if this was the case, a private was sent upstairs to check the truth of the statement).'

Kurt in Onchan camp remembers these roll-calls: 'We had them every day to see that no one was missing. We called them the Matzo-Gasse because they were held in a side-street. We Germans were very strict; we had to stand still. The Viennese were more relaxed. They said, "It doesn't matter." '

'After the morning roll-call,' Jacobsthal continues, 'the daily programme went as follows: lunch at 12.30; tea at 4.00; supper at 6.30, and then another roll-call. Every second day one was bin-carrier. Once every hour, and especially at meal times, a messenger came and brought a slip with communications from the camp administration and mostly forms to be filled in, destined for either the commandant or the self-administration. There were lists to be made of hairdressers, cooks, engineers, scholars, people over and under fifty, practising Jews, Protestants, Catholics, destitutes, holders of bank accounts, people arrived from other camps, chess and bridge-players, people willing to deliver or to attend lectures on everything, people interested in kosher food, men with wives, sisters, daughters or nieces in camps on the isle, or with sons in Canada, people willing to emigrate to America, Canada or Australia, men under fifty ready to enlist in the Pioneers – the longer we stayed, the more numerous became the lists, a symptom of German over-organisation and *Grundlichkeit* [thoroughness] and of growing nervousness.'

This passion for statistics is reflected in a survey of the occupations of internees at Onchan camp published in the *Onchan Pioneer*, their duplicated journal.

'Otherwise', Jacobsthal goes on, 'we were left to ourselves. It goes without saying that there was much *Kultur*. In charge of the *Kulturabteilung* [Culture Department] was a certain Herr Ahrends and each house had a *Kulturwart* [Culture Warden] – in our house poor Pfeiffer – who had to go to a meeting every morning and then to report home. And there was also a board in front of the post-office with the communications of the "Hutchinson Camp University". The lectures in July and August were given on the lawn, overhead seagulls screeching and 'planes droning and roaring, then in a hall over the canteen where, the walls and floor being flimsy, one could listen either to the lecturer or to the arguments downstairs in the canteen. There were some serious and very good lectures by people of our set who deemed it their duty to contribute, among them a masterly lecture by Pfeiffer on English Humanism, forming part of a cycle "Aspects of English Life". But the majority of these lectures were cheap and delivered by dilettantes or conceited scholars.

'Pleasanter and more important for the morale of the internees was the highly respectable musical life. It was moving when fifty unhappy men gathered in one of the narrow shabby rooms and listened to Professor Glas playing Bach, Mozart or Schubert on a worn-out piano, or to Ravicz's masterly, melancholy jazz improvisations.

'I never went to any of the very popular performances of the *Cabaret Stacheldraht*, which had, as I was told, the character of Jewish varieties in certain quarters of Vienna. Some of the English officers went. The internees of some other camp on the isle were tactless enough to offer a public performance for the Manx people, the proceeds of which should be given to the Manx Spitfire Fund. Then somebody seems to have opened their eyes and it was advertised that the money should go to the Red Cross. But it had to be cancelled even in this form and I was on the side of the respectable Manx ladies who for weeks wrote strong letters about tactless aliens to the editor of the *Manx Times*.

'This was the *Kultur* for the *polloi*. The better part of spiritual life was going on in private, unorganised. And No. 24 was the respected and much envied centre. Every night after dinner and roll-call we put our two tables in the common-room together, covered the windows with embezzled blankets and screened the stolen bulb with the bellows of an old photographic camera which Cohn had discovered on a rubbish heap in the basement. Lectures and discussion went on until about 10.15 p.m., when the air-raid warden furiously knocked at the window: "Put your bloody lights out!" For weeks, on every second night, Pfeiffer interpreted the *Odyssey*: for a long time, before the Clarendon Press furnished us with a real classical library and even with a Liddell and Scott Greek dictionary, Beazley's duodecimo *Odyssey* was the only text we had. I was certainly the most grateful among the audience, for I read Homer twice during these months with a pleasure and an intensity as hardly ever before. Our permanent guests were our neighbours Professor Rothfels, Professor Schulz and Dr Bersu, once the director of the Roman–German department of the German Archaeological Institute; also the sculptors Ehrlich and Charoux attended from time to time. Another series of lectures was given by Professor Isaac. He treated his special subject, metabolism. Dr Forchheimer lectured on "Unemployment" and "Trade Cycles"; Wellesz on "Genesis of an Opera" and "Modern Viennese Music"; Dr Loening on "The Technique of Printing". Dr Bersu had a "children's class" in prehistory and once told us the facts of the destruction and reconstruction of the library of Louvain – he had been officially concerned with this problem. Professor Rothfels read to us the introduction to his *Bismarck*, written for the English world. Dr von Klemperer, formerly director-general of Schwartzkopf Ltd, a leading man in German heavy industry, told us something of his work and was rewarded with a diploma. . . .

'These evenings were a serious matter and prevented boredom and pointless talk. I sometimes felt reminded of people on a polar expedition. Sometimes we went to attend lectures in other houses. Professor Goldmann, Professor of Law at the University of Vienna and an authority on Etruscan language, had three classes on "Select Problems of Etruscan Philology". Once Graf Matuschka recited from his poems, noble in sentiment and diction.

'Serious work was also done in a school of engineering, where boys, living together in one house with their teachers, were taught by capable mathematicians and engineers. Of artists, Charoux and

Ehrlich had been leading sculptors in Austria and had lived in Britain for several years. Both had had successful exhibitions in Bond Street. Both made lots of drawings of me and Ehrlich made my bust in plasticine. . . . In return I had a class with them and with Weissenborn on Greek sculpture, looking with them at some good photos in one of those numerous cheap German picture-books of which Ehrlich had a copy. Of the other artists, Uhlmann was the most interesting. . . . In this country he had become the son-in-law of Lord Croft, which had not prevented his internment.

'Social structure: in the camp were normally about 1200 men; accessions from dissolved camps on the mainland roughly equalled the number of releases. The bulk were people between the ages of forty and seventy, but gradually the average age was lowered by the entry of sons or other younger men. Austrians were far more numerous than Germans. 80 per cent of the inmates were Jews. Of these, approximately 150 were orthodox and lodged in kosher houses. Many of them wore little black caps and had the appearance and manners of inhabitants of East European ghettos or the London East End. Many of them did not speak German, but Yiddish or English with a funny accent; it was not always easy to find out what they were really speaking. The majority of them had actually lived before internment in those quarters of London, long before Hitler, but had for reasons of economy or others not applied for naturalisation. Others had quite recently come over from Nazi-invaded countries. A small minority came from Germany. I once saw six of them sitting together in the front garden of a kosher house, all very dignified figures with long beards, and in a wailing voice telling one after the other (in turn) the tale how in those terrible days of November 1938 the synagogue was blown up, the *Torah* profaned. The tale was followed by a chorus, a song or prayer in Hebrew – a pathetic scene. Others were less dignified and had the looks of Balkan house-dealers or Romanian pimps, out of one of Panait Istrati's novels. . . . On the whole the orthodox Jews had their own ways, never attended lectures, concerts and the like, but shuffled endlessly up and down the square, talking and gesticulating or reading their Hebrew holy books. There were many rabbis, and on Saturdays always orthodox and liberal services on the lawn. They also lectured on many problems of Jewish life and culture.

'The Jews knew that they were in the majority. They naïvely took everyone to be of their kind and it was quite common in the first days to be addressed by an unknown man, "How much a week do you get from Bloomsbury House?" Or when I was once waiting for an hour at the gate before I was let out to the parcel department, and reading my duodecimo *Odyssey*, a sympathetic old Jew turned to me and said, "What a nice little Talmud you have." A less pleasant side was that this majority of orthodox and especially non-orthodox Jews suspected all non-Jews as "Nazis" and always tried to push their candidates into the more important camp jobs. Jews are highly unsociable and utterly lacking the virtue of military discipline: at the roll-call they always had their hands in their pockets, and went on talking while the officers counted them. This lasted until the commandant put up a notice on the board, "The roll-call is a parade and the internees have . . . ." It must be no easy job to govern Palestine. It was interesting to me that on the Day of National Prayer the commandant and staff simply attended the Jewish service as that of the majority, and not the Protestant.

'A class worthwhile mentioning is "Aryan" Germans who had lived in England for forty or even fifty years and, like those East End Jews, not applied for naturalisation. Some of them had already had a Manx holiday in 1914–18. Most of these were of lower social standard – waiters, small shopkeepers, artisans, speaking no German at all. Some had sons in HM Forces and one had in 1914–18 been a captain of a merchant cruiser and had a breast full of decorations. He would hardly have been interned had he not driven a car in a state of complete drunkenness and climbed up the post of a street lantern.

'The broad middle stratum of the internees consisted of business-men of every description, most of them most certainly material useful to the economy of any country. They had left Germany after the pogroms of November 1938 and entered this country. 50 per cent of them had been granted a permit to work, the rest, less fortunate, had made preparations for emigration to the United States.

'Of the upper class, I have already introduced some scholars of distinction, but my list must be enlarged by the following names: Dr Haymann, once Professor of Law at the University of Cologne; Dr Misch, professor at the University of Göttingen; Dr W. Cohn, keeper of Oriental Antiquities in the Ethnographical Museum of Berlin; Professor Fehr of Berlin, an ophthalmologist of international reputation. . . . There were dozens and dozens of barristers, doctors, engineers, Catholic and Protestant ministers, leading industrialists, bankers, and so on.

'So far I have tried to give an unprejudiced record of facts. Now I should like to speak of problems and atmosphere, no less important for an understanding of this episode. Confinement is more than loss of freedom in the sense that the space of movement is narrowed. I personally have never suffered from the barbed wire as others did. I was quite content to sit in the sun on the lawn and to read Homer, and every second day I took part in one of the walks across the beautiful country with lots of sentries and bayonets watching us, just for hygienic reasons. Nor have I ever complained of the conditions, different indeed from those at home, less still when the *Blitzkrieg* started and so many Britishers had to stand hardships far worse than we in this place without air-raids. Confinement means a break in the continuity of existence, an interruption of the normal flux of life. It causes trauma: the natural relation and proportional importance of present, past and future become distorted. Suddenly, through the repression of the present, the past creeps up, assuming gigantic dimensions and occupying an unproportionally large field of conscious life. And, while a man sentenced to imprisonment of a clearly defined period can tell how many days, weeks or months he has still before him, in our particular case there was absolute uncertainty. Were we locked up for the duration of the war? Would we be out soon, after a fortnight? After two months? Three months? Would we still be here at Christmas? Would we be deported to Canada?

'Another aspect of confinement is the loss of contact with the world outside. In Hutchinson camp we were allowed to subscribe to newspapers: we regularly read *The Times*, the *Daily Telegraph*, the *Manchester Guardian*, the *Manx Times* and, before this was forbidden by new regulations, the *New Statesman* and *Picture Post*. But I seriously and most strongly complain of the cruel, scandalous treatment of our mail. For over three weeks my wife did not know where I was, and I, having been interned on 5 July, had the first message from her on 30 July, none of our letters and wires ever having been delivered. It was no different with the correspondence of other people. We were allowed to write twice a week twenty-four lines on specially prepared paper. These letters were censored in Liverpool and arrived after about a fortnight or up to twenty days. Letters from home, also going via Liverpool, occasionally censored in the camp, took a week, so that at least three weeks passed before one had an answer to a question. During the first weeks, extra letters and wires were possible if the urgency of the matter could be proved to the intelligence officer, but the regulations became stricter and stricter and the only exceptions finally were letters to a solicitor. When I had to write in a matter connected with his application for my release to the Dean of Christ Church, this letter had to be directed to a solicitor who then communicated with the Dean. In normal times, people correspond about weather, food, the garden or the children or give instructions to their wives to pay or not to pay bills. Here were men whose very existence was at stake, whose sons were deported to Canada, who were making preparations for emigration, who had to dissolve their businesses, had to carry on a regular, ample correspondence with authorities and firms here and abroad, had to inform and consult their families on these steps. A case in which I had to give advice was that of the director of a large technical firm working for ministries whose chairman had sold the machinery and him to a foreign country but he was not in the least able to discuss matters and details with them. It is quite intelligible that after the beginning of the *Blitzkrieg* the wires in this country had to be reserved as much as possible for telegrams of national importance, but why all these restrictions on letters? Why this costly censorship in Liverpool? What could Mr Cohn write to Mrs Cohn in Birmingham that was not common knowledge? Was it really interesting to the censor to know whether he liked or disliked the food or even complained about the Home Office delaying his release? And what interest could the censor take in the stupid letters of Mrs X of Golders Green to her interned husband? The only explanation seems to me that by lack of precedent the authorities simply applied the regulations in force for prisoners of war. The internees were very much embittered and hardly any aspect of internment has done so much harm to the sincere and profound admiration of everything British they had felt before.

'Warth Mill had been a piece of adventure and black romance claiming all one's energies to bear up. Hutchinson camp – only a very few of us noticed it – was far more fantastic. There were those ghastly rows of boarding-houses, and going on in them a life, bourgeois without any hardship, of strangers sentenced to intimacy of meals and bed. It had been much easier to lie on the floor in a hall with 400 people. And the lawn under the always blue summer sky, haunted by idlers, and those ghostlike professors, selling their old German stuff again after the years that they had been muzzled, hardly aware of the weird unreality of their situation. And all this while Liverpool and London were bombed . . . .

'The whole, a "German holiday", a complete relapse, after short and imperfect acclimatisation, into former language and habits, bowing and introduction: "Gestatten Sie . . ."; and people addressing each other "Herr Geheimrat", "Herr Hofrat". The German past, which during the last years had sunk to the bottom of consciousness, came to the surface again. It was pleasant to conjure up reminiscences of childhood and later life, to talk of people and places in Berlin, dear to Loening and Pfeiffer and myself, to call up Göttingen and Marburg, Bonn and Heidelberg, with the eidola of former colleagues with whom we professors had once lived and worked. But there was also a more serious aspect: on our nightly walks round the square, Isaac and I often thought of the loss of *Muttersprache* [mother-tongue] as the saddest part of emigration, or how much of the best part of German learning and teaching remained inactive in diaspora where a scholar had to fit in with an immensely different great tradition. We dreamt of an Utopian scheme, to pull the ugly houses down, to build instead good modern institutes and to open the German Manx University with terms during the Oxford and Cambridge vacations so that advanced people could come here for courses . . . . But where was the Manx millionaire willing to give us a million pounds? Slowly and imperceptibly we lost every feeling of the fantastic unreality of life, of its absurd rhythm and *nomos* [law], and we were hardly still aware that only two months ago we had lived an existence like that of the people we met on our walks in the country. If the beasts in the zoo could speak, they would tell us of similar experiences.'

# 21 The Way Out

No dramatic exodus of internees from the camps followed the publication of the 30 July White Paper.

That the government was prepared to release some of the interned aliens met with almost general acclaim from those involved. It was about the only aspect of the White Paper that did.

Was the Minister aware, asked George Strauss, MP for Norwich, that under the list published Professor Einstein, Toscanini and Thomas Mann would still be in internment camps? Was he aware that the White Paper met with almost universal reprobation? asked Mr Wedgwood, and tabled a motion to that effect forthwith.

The basic weakness in its logic was instantly apparent. The men had been interned because they might imperil national security at a time when the safety of the country was most gravely threatened. Yet those of them who could be useful to the war-effort were being given the opportunity to be released. Were the 'useful' less dangerous? And, conversely, were the 'useless' by definition a menace, to be kept confined? Or were they merely being punished for their uselessness?

'Men should be let out of internment because they are innocent not because they are useful', argued Rhys Davies (Westhoughton, Lancashire) in a big debate on internment in the Commons on 22 August.

'If they are dangerous, keep them in. If they are not dangerous, let them out', stated Mr Wedgwood.

A second weakness in the scheme was the inadequacy and cumbersomeness of the machinery for implementing it. Speaker after speaker in a debate in the House of Lords in mid August emphasised the need for a simpler process of releasing the innocent. 'How is it possible to deal with 30,000 cases with only one or two committees?' asked Lord Mancroft. 'What we wanted was to get innocent people set free who, without doubt, ought not to be locked up. If that is to be done, not one or twenty but fifty committees should be got to work at once.'

Expansion at the Aliens Department of the Home Office was proceeding, replied the Duke of Devonshire for the government. But an immense difficulty was that in most cases it really could not be proved whether a man's sympathies were genuine or not. 'There can be no doubt', he said, 'that there are cases of refugees – people probably with admirable references – who have been sent here by the Nazi government. There can also be no doubt that some of these refugees from Nazi Germany remain German at heart.' It was the earnest desire of the Home Secretary to expedite the business as much as possible, but he had to be satisfied that a given person could be left at large without prejudice to the national interest.

The difficulty of obtaining security clearance did not explain a not untypical case described by Lord Faringdon, of an order for release received six weeks after it was made. The man concerned had been in hell for six weeks. 'Somebody', he raged, 'should be made to smart for mismanagement of this kind.'

And 'incompetence' and 'mismanagement' in connection with the whole internment policy are words which recur during the House of Commons debate on 22 August. 'What may start as incompetence and mismanagement may, if not corrected, very soon become cruelty', warned Major Cazalet. 'I admit that there has been exaggeration. . . . How can you expect that there will not be exaggeration when it has taken over three weeks to get a letter from one party to another . . . when the *Oxford Book of English Verse* has been decreed an unsuitable book for a refugee; when names have been lost; when people have disappeared?' Already at the beginning of the month Sir John Anderson had attributed delay in some releases to 'a certain confusion in the records, which was the result of the haste in which certain measures were taken'.

The House was given at least two examples of such confusion on 1 August, when Mr Wedgwood asked the Home Secretary for information about the whereabouts of an internee, Hans Alec Rosenfelder. He was on the Isle of Man, Sir John replied. But, said Wedgwood, he had received a letter just that morning informing him that Rosenfelder had been deported to Australia. 'There is always', Sir John answered, 'a possibility of confusion.'

A more tragic case was described by J. P. Morris (MP for North Salford), concerning one Horst Giesener, the sixteen-year-old son of a domestic servant living in Salford, who had been interned on 16 May. On 17 July the Home Office agreed that, if the boy's employers signified their willingness to employ him, he would be released. They had done so, but he had not been freed. Letters and parcels sent to him at Huyton had been returned; prepaid telegrams to the camp had received no reply. A telephone message to the camp elicited the information that his name was not on the list of internees, and that he had probably been sent overseas. 'This boy', said Sir John, 'volunteered to go to Australia and embarked on 10 July.'

On 12 August an Information Bureau was opened at St Stephen's House, London to enable families and friends to trace the whereabouts of those who had disappeared into the maw of internment. A Central Index was set up there for this purpose. An initial rush of several hundred inquiries a day soon caused more complaints of delay and inadequacy.

An unusual objection to government policy came from Captain Alan Graham (MP for Wirral, Cheshire). Could the Home Secretary assure the House he asked, 'that in releasing from British internment camps those who have been hostile to Fascism, he is not releasing those whose devotion to the cause of the Communist world revolution is as great a menace to the peace and institutions of this realm as either Fascism or Nazism?' 'Yes', said Sir John, eliciting a sharp retort from left-wing Willie Gallacher (MP for West Fife): 'Are we to take it from the question and answer that the maintenance of the capitalist system of society, with all its poverty and unemployment and all its institutions, is to continue? This is a shameful business.'

On the positive side, the 22 August debate was the occasion for Sir John Anderson to explain adjustments he was making to the categories for release, while still maintaining a policy of general internment. Most important here was a recommendation by the Asquith Committee that a new category be adopted to cover 'any person as to whom a tribunal, appointed by the Secretary of State for the purpose, reports that enough is known of his history to show that by his writings or speeches or political or official activities he has consistently, over a period of years, taken a public and prominent part in opposition to the Nazi system and is actively friendly towards the Allied cause'.

Other recommendations of the Asquith Committee were also of considerable significance, particularly for the unfortunate 'Bs'. As mentioned, the Regional Advisory Committees charged with reviewing the cases of enemy aliens graded 'B' had barely begun their work when it was interrupted by general internment. The

Asquith Committee felt that the 75 per cent of the total whose cases had not been reheard at that point should have that privilege. They were therefore to be given the opportunity to apply for release from internment if they were eligible under one of the categories in the White Paper. Their cases would then be referred to a tribunal appointed for that purpose which would decide which grade they should be given; if 'C' they would, security considerations permitting, be released.

Moreover, the cases of all 'Bs', the Asquith Committee advised, should be subject to a general revision on grounds of equity. In so far as inclusion in 'B' implied a stigma, that stigma, where appropriate, should be removed, even if there were no question of immediate release.

Thirdly, the Asquith Committee recommended that, when a category 'C' alien was released, special consideration should be given to the question of releasing his wife.

All the Committee's recommendations, said Sir John, had been accepted.

During the same speech he also outlined his plans for the release of Italians who had been interned. Although he had promised that the same arrangements made for Germans and Austrians would extend as far as was applicable to Italians, the fact was that there had been no classification whatsoever of the Italians. He therefore proposed to set up an advisory committee to consider cases of Italian internees who fell within the categories of eligibility and to advise him whether any of them could be regarded as so friendly towards Britain and so sympathetic to the Allied cause that they could safely be released without prejudice to the national interest. The committee would be chaired by Sir Percy Loraine, erstwhile British ambassador in Rome, and consist of persons with special knowledge of Italian politics and life.

The debate on 22 August also gave Osbert Peake the occasion to draw attention to other favourable developments. The intensity of censorship of internees' mail would be relaxed as unnecessary, and this should expedite postal communications. When the Home Office took over the camps on 5 August, he said, it had found nearly 100,000 letters by internees held up by the postal censorship at Liverpool.

All sorts of factors, Peake said, would diminish the internee population: not only the releases through the White Paper, but also recruitment for the Pioneer Corps, which had already begun in the camps, as well as increased emigration overseas. A new quota year for emigration to the United States was beginning and the chances for Germans and Austrians to secure visas were significantly enhanced by the fact that their compatriots still in Germany and Austria would not be competing for them.

Despite this optimism and these innovations the debate brought agitation against the government's internment policy to a new peak. Particular exception was taken to a claim by Lord Winterton, self-styled 'friend' of the refugees, British government representative and chairman of the Evian Committee, that 'after these people were interned there was much less leakage of information from this country to the Continent than before they were interned'.

'The Minister still regards refugees *en masse* rather as potential enemies than as eager friends', commented the *New Statesman*. 'Perhaps his most typical statement on this theme was his endorsement of Lord Winterton's claim. To those who remember that the beginning of the internment policy coincided with the disappearance of half a dozen neutral channels for the transmission of information, to say nothing of the Italian ambassador and his staff, this fact, if it is a fact, is not surprising. Yet no attempt was made to connect it with any instance of a "C" category refugee having attempted to communicate with Germany. Can Lord Winterton or Sir John Anderson produce any real evidence against the refugees?'

Paul Jacobsthal thought not. 'It had been one of the motives given for general internment of male aliens that among them might be spies and fifth-columnists. During those months I talked to hundreds and hundreds of internees, and overheard thousands of talks of people who thought themselves unobserved – and I claim an experience superior to that of any judge or intelligence officer. I should like to state with the greatest emphasis that I have not met a single man liable to the faintest suspicion.'

Other publications attacked other aspects of government internment policy. 'No words are strong enough', wrote *The Economist*, 'to condemn the callousness, the clumsiness and the general incompetence with which the question has been handled.'

'Where is the speed-up?' asked the *News Chronicle*. 'It still takes from ten days to a fortnight for a letter posted in this country to reach an internee in this country. . . . It would be more reassuring if those responsible for the well-being of our internees would see that so elementary a task as that of delivering letters was performed with even moderate efficiency.'

'Public opinion . . . is to continue to be ignored; our prestige abroad, particularly in the United States, is to be lowered; passionate anti-Nazis are still to be detained because the Home Office is incapable of distinguishing them from Nazi agents', claimed the *Spectator*.

The new category appeared as the nineteenth clause of a new White Paper on Internment issued by the government a few days after the debate. 'This rule must have been drafted by some well meaning official who had not the dimmest idea of what life in Nazi Germany was like', wrote H. N. Brailsford in *Reynolds News*. 'No "public" and "prominent" opposition was tolerated for five minutes, but this rule exacts it "over a period of years".'

The clause, the *Jewish Chronicle* feared, was full of snares. The research required to build up a case to obtain the release of just one individual under its terms would be immense.

The members of the tribunal to implement the new clause were announced a few weeks later. The chairman was to be Sir Cecil James Barrington Hurst; other members were Sir Andrew McFadyean, Professor Robert William Seton-Watson and Ivone Augustine Kirkpatrick.

This, the *Manchester Guardian* pointed out, brought the number of advisory committees appointed by the Home Secretary to clear up the 'refugee muddle' to 137, staffed by 494 people. The original tribunals had a judge apiece, a police inspector, and a liaison officer; the regional committees had each a panel of ten or twelve members.

Cheered by the controversy raging around them; appreciative of the fact that the government had found time to discuss their problems, when they had so many very serious problems of their own; clutching at the straws offered – the interned thousands began tirelessly to negotiate their release. The writing of applications became a constant occupation. The following poem conveys the atmosphere of camp life at the time.

IT DOES NOT WORRY ME AT ALL

(first-prize camp hit)

*Music*: Bleier                                        *Text*: Wally

Roll Call; Everybody out for Roll Call!
Cover up those blue pyjamas,
'Cause you didn't dress at all.
Roll Call! Have a look at sand and water,
Maybe you can spot a mermaid
From the Mooragh Promenade.
So fall in everybody, and please form up four deep
Until they have finished counting the asses and the sheep.
Roll Call! Every morning it gets later,
But I'm doing them the favour,
IT DOES NOT WORRY ME AT ALL.


Porridge! Every morning we have porridge
Sometimes thick and sometimes liquid,
People eat it after all.
Porridge! Keeps you slim and fit and happy,
As to me – to make it snappy –
I don't eat the stuff at all.
I save it up for Adolf for use after this war
When he takes up his old job: hanging paper on the wall.
Porridge! Every morning I taste porridge,
Just for doing them the favour,
IT DOES NOT WORRY ME AT ALL.


Blackout! In the evening there is blackout.
Mind you blackout every window.
Don't show a light – however small
Blackout! Can't you hear the sentries crying,
When in bed you're softly lying:
'Put that bloody light out there.'
How would you like a bomb dear, drop right on top of you?
You sure would have a headache and maybe, flat feet too.
Blackout! Let us see to our blackout,
'Cause it goes in our favour,
AND DOES NOT WORRY US AT ALL.

Application! Have you made your application?
Never mind if you come under
Any paragraph at all.
Application is the road to your salvation.
Have no fear, no hesitation –
Unless you are quite happy here.
Myself, I did not bother, I'm going soon enough
I want to be in khaki, on Hitler I'll be rough.
Application is the road to YOUR salvation,
Only please – do ME one favour:
AND DO NOT WORRY ME AT ALL.

PS.  Romance! Are you starved of love and romance?
Are you looking for an outlet
For your masculinity?
Romance! Twice a week – perhaps more often –
Would relieve your indigestion
And make your kidneys work with glee.
'Round here there are no women, no cinemas, no girls,
So I look at Marischka, who's got such lovely curls.
Romance! I need FUN and LOVE and ROMANCE,
But who's doing me the favour????
Nobody in this Camp at all????

Paul Jacobsthal writes in a more sober vein about the same period: 'After July the atmosphere became worse and worse and the camp seethed with anger and excitement. People now learned from letters how many of their friends in London, "C" class aliens like themselves, had not been interned, with no sensible reason given for such discriminate treatment. My neighbour, Herr N, the owner of a large shoe-factory employing 350 British workers, rightly said, "They lock me up and that creature, Herr A who has just come over and has nothing to live on is at large." But why speak of Herr N? They had interned in Oxford all university people, but had left out a German dentist because of his useful work. Our answer was, "Are dentists believed to be *a priori* politically trustworthy?" For, after all, internment was a political measure. People hardly talked about anything else but release, release, they were *himmelhoch jauchzend* or *zu Tode betrübt* [on top of the world, or in the depths of despair] according to their naïve interpretation of which pro- or anti-aliens articles they had read. They made application after application and tried to pull wires, severely hampered by the restrictions on correspondence. I felt like a scribe in the orient, writing letters for the *agraphoi* [illiterate]. To avoid contagion I stopped my ears and brought to perfection the art of reading Homer without listening to the babble. The situation became clearer and the tension relaxed when the Home Office published a White Paper stating eighteen categories of people whose release would be considered. But people were clever enough to see its weak spot: "They intern us as fifth-columnists and spies and release us because we are over sixty-five, sick, agricultural workers, employers of twelve British subjects, and so on." But these reflections did not prevent them from writing fresh applications and from pestering the camp doctor with their real or imaginary ailments. In August the release machinery was set going, slowly, five people or fewer leaving every day. The order in which they came out and sometimes the reasons why were utterly unapparent. One day, a sick man and a rabbi, the next, an old man and one in whom a bishop took an interest, another rabbi, then an agricultural worker, a boy employed by the Royal Automobile Club and a destitute who was sorry to leave and did not know on what he was going to live. Of our set, only Professor Weigert, the chemo-physicist, was early released, either because his work was considered to be of national importance or because the Home Office had satisfied itself that a man who is stone deaf would hardly be able to communicate with parachutists; and Professor Paul Maas, useful indeed as the co-editor of Liddell and Scott. Our attitude was cynical. We had in mind a cartoon by Low: Sir John Anderson turning a specially constructed tombola and a mixed lot jumping out of it at random. Our greatest delight was the elephant-keeper of a zoo, who had been the first to be released from Paignton internment-camp because the pregnant elephant did not take food from another keeper. I asked myself: would my pupils take their food from another man?'

Ulrich Skaller was one of those released in August: 'After the parliamentary debate in July our situation improved: we in Huyton were allowed newspapers; a canteen was installed where we could buy food and other small articles – handkerchiefs, whatever you needed – at reasonable prices. We could receive parcels and, most important of all, we were cheered by the news that machinery was being set up to sort us out. I was one of the first to be sorted out and by mid August I could go to London, but not back to Leigh-on-Sea, which was a protected area.'

Pastor Ehrhardt was also released from Huyton at around this time, in his case on grounds of ill health. So too was Batya Emanuel's brother, though for different reasons. 'My brother was released after several applications by my mother (a law had come out that people under eighteen could be released). He was released into the custody of his parents – which always amused me as one of his parents was still in an internment-camp. It was rather odd!'

Julius Carlebach 'volunteered for the Army in order to get out of the camp but they told me I was too young; I was only seventeen. And then, quite abruptly, after two or three weeks I was released. Apparently after intervention by a few people, the government had agreed to release the under-eighteens.'

The release of 1687 aliens was authorised during August. About one tenth of category 'C' aliens who had been interned had by then been released, the Duke of Devonshire told the House of Lords, and cases of nearly double that number were under consideration.

During the period of these early releases a new, but short-lived, cause for concern came to light. Why, asked Rhys Davies, were aliens released from internment requested to sign a promise to the authorities not to describe, under penalty of being interned again, the conditions prevailing in their camps? The *Manchester Guardian* threw partial light on this claim on the basis of interviews with three internees from different camps, all of whom spoke good English. All agreed that they were told to make the promise verbally at their interviews with their respective camp commandants at the time of their release, at the same time as they were asked to sign a receipt for their personal belongings.

Sir John Anderson put paid to the practice in any form. 'I caused an instruction to be sent to all the camps that nothing is to be said or done to suggest that there is the least desire, so far as the camp authorities are concerned, to place any restriction on what an alien may say or write about the condition in camps after he had been set at liberty.'

On 31 August German bombers flew for the first time over the Isle of Man – one of the rare occasions when the air-raid instructions issued to internees had some relevance. The mainland was not so fortunate. On 15 August Hitler launched 'Operation Eagle', intended to bomb Britain into surrender, before 'Operation Sealion', the naval invasion, could take place.

Although the camp at Huyton was situated near to heavily bombed Liverpool, no air-raid shelters were available there, and the small estate houses offered no protection against bombs, or even blast and splinters.

Batya Emanuel's father was moved from Huyton to nearby Whiston hospital. 'They X-rayed him lots of times and could find nothing organically wrong, because worrying about your family is not an illness, and he could not be released because there was no illness to put down. There was lots of bombing there because it was near Liverpool, and the patients were ordered when there was an air-raid to get out of bed and lie under the bed because it was safer. My father did it once, and after that he decided that, as it was dark, they could not possibly see who was in, and who was under, the bed, and he personally would rather die in bed.'

# 22 Alien Corn

In Canada, Eugen Spier read the reports of the 22 August debate out loud by a dim light to his crowded hut in a camp on the shores of Lake Superior.

'This was indeed a great moment for every one of us', he wrote. 'Great silence and deep emotion filled the atmosphere of our hut. . . . I felt that the climax of confusion had been reached and already overcome and a definite turn for better and gradually improving conditions was at hand.'

As information regarding the treatment of the internees in Canada percolated through to Britain, their case was being well aired in the House of Commons. Most important perhaps, it was stated that arrangements had been made for Britain to retain responsibility for authorising the release of civilian internees sent to the Dominions. The Home Secretary proposed to review their cases as soon as possible. Arrangements would be made to bring back to Britain at the British government's expense any person whose release was authorised, unless the Dominion government was prepared to allow him to be at large in the Dominion, and he himself desired to stay there.

On 22 August some 212 wives and children of interned aliens waited excitedly in London for permission to join their husbands in Australia. They had, so Eleanor Rathbone alleged, been brought there at the request of the Home Office. Osbert Peake explained the position: a number of married internees had volunteered to go to Australia on a ship which left on 10 July. They were told not that they would be accompanied by their wives but that if possible arrangements would be made for their wives to follow should they be willing to do so. Unfortunately, completion of the arrangements had had to be deferred pending further communication with the Australian government.

'Twice', Jakob Felsenstein says, 'my wife, together with the wives of other internees, was told to be ready to travel to Australia. My wife quit her job. Others disposed of their furniture. All packed their possessions. On both occasions they were informed on the day prior to departure that the ship due to take them had been bombed in Liverpool harbour. So they stayed in England.'

On 22 August, HMS *Dunera* was on the high seas between Capetown and Fremantle. Jakob Felsenstein and the 2000 or so other internees on board were oblivious of the changes that had occurred over the past weeks. Nor was there much indication of these changes when they were disembarked at Sydney on 6 September after a journey of almost two months.

'I was lucky enough to watch the entire spectacle,' writes Klaus Loewald, 'for one of my friends who had the duty to watch over kitchen supplies, took me to his storeroom, where I had a port-hole to myself. As I recall it, we disembarked in the afternoon. Several long trains were ranged along the docks. I remember the apparently giant Australian soldiers who directed us to the carriages, their easy-going attitudes, their surprise at seeing us break into a run automatically when in the open air, and many of the internees who, misinterpreting the waving arms which intended to indicate that there was no need to hurry, ran even faster in their continuing fear of uniformed men.'

'The troops who received us on the train', Felsenstein says, 'soon saw what kind of people we were. There were some veterans among them from the First World War who had even served in Palestine and had smatterings of Hebrew. They said, "Bavakasha shev" [Please sit down]. They were very friendly. They told us that the instructions they had had from the Home Office were to expect dangerous prisoners and be sure to be fully armed and very careful how they approached them. They said, "We can't understand why you were shipped here. Jewish refugees just like you are going around free in Sydney and Melbourne. You also will soon be free. You can settle in Australia. It's a good country." The Australian government had a different point of view and would not let anyone leave the camp and settle. The Australians behaved correctly and were even quite friendly, though they showed their usual characteristics of drinking and swearing.'

Other deported internees were struck by other new experiences. Klaus Loewald, for example: 'The train began to move and we eventually travelled out of Sydney and into a novel kind of landscape which could have been vaguely familiar to those who had seen the more arid parts of California; in other words, to practically none of us. . . . The train stopped at Moss Vale, where each of us received a neat grey carton containing sandwiches and fresh fruit. We ate what we considered to be the most delicious meal imaginable. On board ship, health foods had consisted of an apple and a sip of lime juice per week.'

'The guards put their rifles in the corner', said Felix Darnbacher. 'For twenty-four hours we rode in the train with enormously wide carriages, from Sydney to Hay. It was breath-taking: the sheer size of the country; the enormous distances; twenty-four hours in a train! Through the windows we saw kangaroos hopping around and budgerigars in the skies like starlings.'

'When we arrived in Hay,' Felsenstein relates, 'there was a very impressive parade by us from the railway station to the camp. We had one *Sefer Torah* which a carter, a great, strong chap, had saved from the small place in Austria where he had lived. As we got off the train at Hay we arranged that this co-internee should walk with the *Sefer* at the head of the parade, and, to the accompaniment of our singing of synagogue and Zionist songs, he was the first to go through the gates of Hay, with its barbed wire and watch-towers (it was fashioned on similar lines to a concentration camp). It was a very hot day. We brought with us also the pieces of luggage torn open by the rifles of the British soldiers. We exhibited these on poles. At first, the Australian commander and the soldiers would not believe us, but the evidence was too strong: they had to accept what we said.'

And Rudi Guttman adds, 'The camp consisted of huts and barbed wire. There were bunks in the huts and blankets. We were about twenty-four to a hut.'

'Hay was originally occupied by Italians', another internee says, 'and was a ghost town founded by gold-miners. There were army-type huts made of eucalyptus timber. We slept on bunks with steel netting. We were given shirts and the like. People in the camp elected their own officers for contact with the authorities. We did our own cooking and our own maintenance. It was a well-run enterprise and fairly clean. Now and then someone dug up cigarettes buried by the Germans or Italians. We made our own soap and we also made our own food: smoked mutton, fruit – there was sufficient and wholesome food.'

'It was a half-finished camp', Darnbacher continues. 'I spent the next year there. The cleaning party immediately started cleaning the camp. I worked in the kitchen, which was a great boon because food was short. There were no physical means of making bread. They had been told to expect Italian prisoners of war and they had got in large quantities of spaghetti. We were very hungry: food had been so short on the boat. Some people suffered from scurvy. To try and smuggle a carrot out of the kitchen for my father was a major operation, because people stood around watching. They had nothing else to do. I had to dish out the food equally. At night I dreamt of open mouths. The food later improved beyond all conception. We had lamb chops for breakfast, and eggs. Then we ate very well.'

It was not so simple for the orthodox Jews in the party – Jakob Felsenstein, for example: 'The kosher-living groups were mostly in camps 7 and 8 and had their own specific difficulties. The food was according to the Geneva Convention and like rations for soldiers, which meant that mutton was plentiful because it was cheap. As we could not eat the mutton we had to live on eggs, and two eggs were the equivalent of a kilo of meat in price. We were also given some vegetables and bread and potatoes and rice – starchy food in conditions of great heat and with very little opportunity to work it off with exercise. We applied to the commanding officer that he should send two *shochetim* [ritual slaughterers] who were in our camp to the local slaughterhouse so that we could have a normal diet. He said this was impossible. This was only put right when the Chief Justice of New South Wales, Dr Jordan, came as an official visitor. The kosher-living group put their case to him and he turned to the commanding officer and said, "What these people say seems very reasonable. Why can't it be done?" The major grew red in the face and within a few days we had ample supplies of mutton. Australia had appointed Dr Jordan official visitor to the camp after we had refused to see the Swiss consul, as we did not wish to have anything to do with a representative of the German government even if he himself was Swiss. We did, however, accept a large parcel of second-hand clothing which the Red Cross sent us, as this was not a German gift.

'The Jewish Welfare Board in Sydney sent us different dishes for milk and meat. Before our *shochetim* were allowed to slaughter for us, and when the kosher-living group experienced real hardship, they offered to send us kosher tinned stuff, but we refused, saying, "It's the duty of the British government to feed us." The Jewish community in Sydney sent Mr Brand of the Welfare Board and we also had visits from Rabbi Falk and another rabbi.

'Shortly after we arrived, there appeared a venomous article about us in a Sydney newspaper. We were described as "dangerous Nazis" and there were vivid descriptions of an alleged revolt by us on the ship. I learned later that in the aft of the ship the Nazis had planned some sort of rebellion but that it had been subdued. On the fore sub-deck where we lived with some 2000, mainly Jewish, refugees, there never was a rebellion. The writer of the article also said that we had set fire to objects on the sub-deck. It was all a lie. What had happened was that somebody had put a piece of cloth over our not very bright lamp, our only light, so that it should not disturb his sleep. The heat of the lamp seems to have singed the cloth.

'While we were in Hay we continued and extended and put method into the lecture course we had started on the *Dunera*. Many young people prepared themselves for exams and spent their time in a very useful way. In the confined circumstances we did not do much exercise, but some of us went in for what is now called jogging and we had other physical activities. We were sometimes allowed under guard to go to the nearby river and bathe. That was very delightful. There were beautiful eucalyptus trees growing near the river which we could not see from the camp.'

'I played a lot of football and handball and did a lot of sport generally', says Rudi Guttman. 'When the rainy season came and we were flooded out in the camp, we had to start digging channels to get the water out. I began to get sepsis under my fingernails and I had to have them off in the infirmary. It was run by our own doctors but they had no anaesthetics.

'A canteen was opened in the camp. I had no money – I had no one to send me any – so I got a job in the kitchen. My first job was peeling potatoes. I peeled a whole sack of potatoes a day by hand and I was paid for this.'

Felix Darnbacher's father was made camp canteen-manager. 'It was a very important function. He was one of the few who had contact with the outside world. They all trusted him. He kept the books well.'

Other people did other work. Jakob Felsenstein was 'the assistant spokesman for the kosher-living group and therefore belonged to the internees' administration. In addition, I wrote letters in English for internees who could not write English, and made their application to emigrate to the United States, and so on. I was kept fully occupied with this. Of course, it was all honorary. It was very interesting work.'

'Then it got very, very hot', says Rudi Guttman. 'The Australians have a saying that "Hell is hot, but Hay is a hell of a lot hotter." During the hot weather we used to go and sit on the floor of the shower just to while away the time. Then I got ill. I had rheumatic fever and was hospitalised for a couple of months. The old prison in the town of Hay had been turned into a hospital for the internees. It was fantastic: it was very old and the walls were very thick, so that it was cool inside. The doctors there were Australians.'

While Rudi Guttman was in hospital, preparations were begun for the celebration of the Jewish festival of Passover by the religious internees. 'We were not sure whether we would get *Haggadoth* [Passover prayer-books] for *Pesach* [Passover]', remembers Felsenstein. 'A very gifted young fellow, Oscar Lewin, wrote out on stencils the major part of the *Haggadah*. Between 1936 and 1939 I had sold duplicating machines in London so I knew about these methods. I duplicated the major part of the *Haggadah*. We had a canteen which was profitable and well supervised and we used the profits from this to buy the things we needed. In the end, *Haggadoth* arrived from the Jewish Welfare Board at Sydney. They also sent kosher wine, although we had soaked grapes to make our own, and *matza* [unleavened bread]. We therefore had an excellent *Seder* [Passover service].'

'We made all sorts of petitions to the High Commissioner,' Guttman continues, 'asking to be sent back to England. We took all sorts of signed statements from people about what had happened on the ship. They were sent to the High Commissioner and on to London. We heard that a court-martial was to be held. We asked that some of our people be sent back to England to give evidence. The government obviously decided to get it over as soon as possible and sweep it under the carpet.'

Felsenstein corroborates and elaborates this: 'We also sent complaints to the *Manchester Guardian* and to Colonel Wedgwood, Eleanor Rathbone and Major Cazalet. At first, these were censored, but eventually they got through. One result of this was that the major and a sergeant who had broken bottles on the deck of the *Dunera* so that we would injure our feet were put before a court and sent to prison. So there were rays of hope. Among our complaints was that we had been sent to this forsaken place, dusty and stormy, where there were occasionally even scorpions. Our complaints resulted in Mr Layton being sent out. He must have had a shock when he saw our condition. He obviously had some influence because we were then transferred to a camp where the climate was good.'

But by then it was already May 1941.

# 23 Holy Wedlock

One of the most grievous hardships endured by internees, of either sex, was the separation from their spouses. Even in the Isle of Man, which housed both men and women, contact between male and female camps was at first strictly forbidden and letters from one to the other could not go direct.

Hence the sensational quality of a meeting between husbands and wives on 26 July to decide on deportation to a Dominion.

'In July I saw Freda for the first time since our separation on 15 May', Kurt told me. 'We were given thirty minutes with 5000 other couples. It was a reunion – fantastic! It was an open-air meeting and the weather was fine. I took Freda a rose, which we still keep as a talisman. We had to make up our minds whether to go overseas, presumably to Australia. But the *Arandora Star* tragedy had happened just before. We said that we would only go on condition that we were free on board ship and free in Australia – which they would not guarantee. There were heart-breaking scenes when couples parted again. In the meantime, the doctor advised Freda not to go overseas.'

Marie and Otto Neurath also enjoyed such a reunion: 'It was a great excitement seeing Otto. We were then not married. Otto had lost his wife in 1937. He had become a conquered German and, though living in Holland, would have had to ask permission in Germany to marry me as I am not Jewish. Otto was shown on his passport as a married man and he did not say I was not his wife, so he came. They marched in in alphabetical order. He came in beaming with delight. We spent a wonderful afternoon on the beach. The object of the meeting was to decide whether we would go overseas. We quickly decided "no". The As, Bs, Cs and Ds had a long talk from Joanna Cruickshank about why they should go. We, the Ns, were spared.'

Later such meetings were put on a regular footing. Edith Jacobus, a married woman in Port Erin internment-camp, tells of these meetings: 'The married women were finally allowed to meet their husbands. We were taken by train to Onchan, where there was a big dance-hall. We were watched like prisoners by soldiers with rifles. It was very dramatic, after several months, meeting our husbands. It was also very sad. My husband was a real family man and he had got the news of the deaths of his family in Europe while he was interned.'

The unmarried men, looking on, were also impressed by the event; Heinz Kiewe, for example: 'Occasionally, husbands were allowed to see their wives. They left in companies under guard and some of them moved us very deeply, because on their first trip they picked any flowers they could find to give to their wives.'

'The women in Port Erin', says the young Henry Prais, 'were visited by their husbands. We had access to a meadow and they used to go and pick these incredible bunches of flowers to take to their wives. It was terribly funny; we had to laugh; they picked dandelions and things.'

'The married men used to go and visit the women', Chaim Rabin remembers. 'They went out in the morning and returned in the evening. Some of the young men discovered that they had "aunts" in the women's camps – only these aunts were very pretty girls. The married men came back with photographs and handed them round. Then the young man would suddenly discover that he had an "aunt". The number of people who went on the arranged visits grew and grew. The camp authorities decided that so many people were going and so many buses were needed, and so on, that, if any more wanted to go, they would stop the service. So the married men got busy, and there were no more "aunts".'

'Later', says Marie Neurath, 'engaged people were allowed to meet and then everyone was engaged. Rosy Hahn was engaged to a pianist. The English got wise, so for a few times Otto and I were not allowed to meet, but after we had exchanged a promise of marriage we were allowed to meet again.'

She was reminded of this promise shortly. Early in October the special advisory committee for reclassifying 'B' category internees whose cases had not previously been reviewed by a regional advisory committee was in session in the Isle of Man, under the chairmanship of Sir Robert Dummett, Chief Magistrate of the Metropolitan Police Courts. For the purposes of this new committee, interned refugees who had arrived in Britain after the invasion of Norway and Denmark and had never been classified were regarded as 'Bs'. Marie Neurath was such a case.

'They took our promise of marriage very seriously. When we had a tribunal at Douglas we were asked together, not only on the same day but at the same meeting. The nice thing was that they even tested me about this promise. What would I do if Dr Neurath went to America? I would go to America. What would I do if Dr Neurath stayed in England? I would stay. When had I been in Germany for the last time? 1932. We both got "C".'

Kurt and Freda came into the same category. Kurt says, 'I was called to a tribunal and asked, "Why did you leave Holland when Hitler came?" I told them my views. They agreed. There were half a dozen people there. "What about Freda?" they asked, because they thought she was Christian. There was no "J" in her passport and she does not look Jewish. But we convinced them. They gave us "C" then. Hurray! We were declared "friendly aliens".

'Once when a fellow prisoner was going to a tribunal we wrote letters to our wives on toilet-paper. He would give them to his wife and she would distribute them to the other women. We did not like the idea of sending letters to our wives which took a week to reach them. This chap was caught with thousands of bits of toilet-paper in his pocket and put in prison. We collected ten shillings to buy his wife flowers, as she was in prison too. Our camp commandant convened a meeting of all the offenders and said, "Scotland Yard is going through all the messages now. I don't know if you intend to stay in England after the war, but this will be a black spot on your record for ever." My note said, "We have some pincers here. We'll cut through the barbed wire and fetch you and go on a boat to Ireland."'

Because his wife, Freda, was pregnant, Kurt was not as dependent on the regular meetings nor the tribunals to see her: 'I had special privileges to visit Freda in between the regular visits, with a fixed-bayonet guard.

'On 31 October 1940, the baby was born. I was allowed to see her, again with a fixed-bayonet guard. I got a coat from the quartermaster because it was cold by then. It was the finest nursing home you have ever seen.'

Freda: 'I had a room to myself . . . .'

Kurt: 'And the King paid for it.'

Freda: 'I started labour four days before she was born, and they took me to hospital. The hospital was beautiful, high on a hill in Douglas. But unfortunately my English was not very good, so half the time I did not know what they wanted me to do. I could not understand what they were saying to me. They said, "Push", and I began to laugh. I thought they meant something completely different. They said "Push" again. I thought it meant to pass water. I said, "I can't."

'Evie was born and they were really fantastic. I was there a fortnight. Evie was born during the night and the next morning Kurt came with a suitcase full of chocolate. I thought he had escaped. I was petrified. But the people in his house had collected 18s. 6d. for him and he had gone with a soldier to buy it.'

Kurt: 'I had been brought to the hospital by a soldier with a rifle. I said to him, "I'll be late tonight. You just sit here." And the soldier just sat there, in the hospital, all day. Officially, I was not allowed to go and see Freda, but Sergeant Collins arranged for me to go.'

Freda: 'After about a fortnight I went back to my hotel. I had nothing for the child – not even nappies. They told me they would give me nappies in hospital. When I came back to the hotel I got a room of my own for Evie and me. They took me up to my room and the table was laden with presents: it was full of nappies, little jackets, romper-suits. Each one of the seventy women in the hotel had knitted or bought something, and they had also collected money to buy a little fire for my room.

'They were all waiting eagerly for the new baby to arrive. There was a young girl there of about twenty and she took over Evie immediately, washed and bathed her, and so on. I took Evie out every day but I had no pram, so some of the other internees lent me theirs for a couple of hours every day. When one of the women was released, she left me her pram. It was a horrible pram, all patched up, but it was fantastic for me.

'Afterwards I was completely happy. I talked to Evie as if she were grown-up. I was not alone any more. It was fantastic.'

Not every internee had a new baby for company, but in September many were reunited with children that they had not seen for months. Dr H. writes, 'It was a great joy when the children, left behind at the time of their mothers' internment, finally arrived in Port Erin.' Mothers wept with delight, recorded the *News Chronicle*, as youngsters flung themselves into their arms.

'The blackest day', Dr H. continues, 'was when some of the internees had to be informed by the commandant that their husbands had been drowned when the *Arandora Star* was torpedoed.'

Despite these two extremes, agitation for a mixed camp rumbled on. Already during the 10 July debate Osbert Peake had told the

House that he was trying to arrange for married couples, especially older people, to be together. Why especially older people? he was asked. Was he afraid that they would breed? Sir Edward Grigg, during the same debate, explained that it had not been possible to bring men and women with families together, but that the War Office was trying to put fathers, sons and brothers into the same camps.

Marie Neurath wrote a musical play on the theme of the mixed camp: 'Several plays were put on, Schubert's *Drei Mädel*, for example. In our house there was a girl who knew Persian and Persian literature. She told me exactly the story of *Turandot* in every detail. She gave me the backbone. She was also most interested in making the costumes, and she selected beautiful gramophone records for the music. I had Rosy Hahn, who sang wonderfully, and also a teacher who taught me how to act: don't move your hands, stand still, and so on. We learned something about play-acting, and it gave us great pleasure. We chose the heroine because she was the only girl with a beautiful evening-dress with her. We did it in our house, then in the great hotel.'

In the latter half of October Osbert Peake reminded the House that releases were taking place from both the male and the female camps in a steady flow, that the review of 'B' grade would probably result in the release of still more and that until the scope of the accommodation required could be gauged it would be very difficult to plan for a mixed camp.

By 15 October, about 5000 German, Austrian and Italian internees had been released since the publication of the White Paper. Some 14,000 remained in camps in the United Kingdom and the Isle of Man, 85 per cent of them in the Isle of Man.

By that date Paul Jacobsthal was already back in Oxford: 'On 28 September I was informed by the commandant that I should be released. I knew from a most reliable source that the order for my release had been signed by the Home Secretary longer than a fortnight before, but, as in other cases, it took two weeks until the instructions to the camp authorities were issued. After having gone through the usual formalities, filling in of manifold papers and search of luggage and body, I left on Monday 30 September. This time on board the steamer I paid my extra fare of five shillings and enjoyed myself in the first class. In Liverpool the sirens sounded welcome. At midnight, near Bletchley, when the train without lights crept through the beautiful starry night – it was new moon –

towards Oxford, I saw for the first time the firework of shells over London. In Oxford I walked from the London Midland Scottish station to the police to report and then past Christ Church and Carfax down home on old familiar paths, this time not driven in the Black Maria.'

Peter Katz was released in October: 'In my case it was my school which applied to take me into residence. I had been interned nineteen weeks. It was the first time I was away from home really, and also the first time I met a cross-section of people. I can look back on it with humour, but the worrying part was the state of the war and the fact that I was separated from my parents.'

'Because I was in agriculture and there was a great need for agricultural workers,' Henry Berg says, 'I was let out in October 1940 and sent back to the farm. I was even given permission to own a bicycle.'

Eugen Glueckauf was released at that time at the request of the Meteorological Office.

Lastly, Ernst Manasse in Scotland: 'One day I had a letter from Irena, my wife, telling me that my farmer had made an application for me to be released from internment and he would take me back on his farm. On the evening before *Yom Kippur* [the Day of Atonement], 1940, I was told I was released. I asked the rabbi (there were several rabbis in the camp), "Can I travel on *Yom Kippur* or should I wait another day?" So he said I could travel. He knew that I was not pious. The commandant offered me a lift in his car to go to the harbour in Lochgilphead to catch the boat to Ardrossan.' Thirty-six hours later he was home. 'Who enjoyed it most that I had come back? It must have been my dog, because in his joy he peed all down my trousers!'

# 24 Under New Management

On 8 October 1940, Herbert Morrison took over the Home Office. Sir John Anderson, steady, painstaking, conscientious, unpopular, was kicked upstairs to become Lord President of the Council. It was left to Aneurin Bevan to speak the final words of condemnation: 'The Right Honourable Gentleman's handling of the internment of aliens was, and remains, a disgrace to the country. There are many examples of the appalling consequences of the way in which that matter has been managed. . . . Even now the categories of aliens still in internment are a disgrace to the country . . . .'

The *Jewish Chronicle* was characteristically optimistic about the change: 'Mr Morrison's presence at the Home Office will, it is believed, result in an extension of the categories for exemption and a more liberal interpretation of existing conditions for release.'

This time the *Chronicle* was not to be disappointed. A new White Paper appeared on 17 October announcing three new categories under which application for release could be made. They involved certain persons eminent in art and learning (category 20), certain categories of students (21), and certain categories of people who had lived for at least twenty years in the United Kingdom (22). Cases coming under this last category would be considered by the same tribunal, headed by Sir Cecil James Barrington Hurst, as decided on those under category 19. Nine *ad hoc* committees to deal with applications under categories 8 and 20 would be appointed by the Royal Society, the British Academy, the Vice-Chancellor of Oxford University, the Committee of Vice-Chancellors, the Royal Academy, the Royal Institute of British Architects, the PEN Club, Dr Ralph Vaughan Williams and the Right Honourable Justice Scott.

On 22 October a further positive step was signalled when Osbert Peake announced that a representative of the United Kingdom government was being sent to Canada at the request of the Canadian government to assist them in dealing with the internees deported there from Britain. He was Alexander Paterson, MC, one of His Majesty's Commissioners of Prisons in England and Wales. Paterson, who arrived in Canada on 19 November, was charged with selecting suitable applicants for the Pioneer Corps and also men who appeared to come within the other categories of eligibility for release.

Despite these two important developments, discontent rumbled on. There were troubles in the British camps themselves. On 1 November, Signor Cosomati, a well-known cartoonist, was attacked and severely beaten by two Fascist fellow-internees in the Palace internment-camp on the Isle of Man. Cosomati's anti-Mussolini cartoons had recently been reprinted in the English Sunday press. The camp authorities held an enquiry and two internees were sentenced to twenty-one days' detention in cells for having instigated the attack. The incident brought to light rumours of Fascist intimidation within the camp. The internees, it was said, were completely under the domination of an aggressive Fascist minority who had appointed themselves to all posts of responsibility, threatened those who volunteered for the Pioneer Corps, and intimidated all who did not share their Fascist sympathies. On 14 November a new camp was opened at Douglas, making segregation of Fascist elements possible.

Not all problems could be solved with such apparent smoothness. Mr Wedgwood, taking clever advantage of a debate on 7 November on a government proposal to increase aid to the voluntary organisations responsible for the German refugees, aired his condemnation of the policy as a whole. The increased sum should not be voted because it would enable the government's internment policy to continue. 'If these people were not interned, they would at the present time be able to support their families', he said. And, later in the same speech: 'We do not want charity, neither do the internees. They do not want your £375,000: what they want is justice.' (The increased sum was voted.)

The attack was given added ammunition by the publication at approximately this time of two books, *The Internment of Aliens*, by Francis Lafitte (a Penguin Special), and *Anderson's Prisoners*, by 'Judex' (a Gollancz 'Victory Book'). Both were heavy indictments of government policy. Neither spared gruelling detail of the suffering and hardship it had caused.

More specific criticism of the White Paper itself was contained in a document dated 5 November, drawn up by a group of internees in

Central Promenade camp, Isle of Man: 'There is no category and therefore no hope of release, for the ordinary man. A man who is neither scientist, priest, rabbi, key-man, too young, too old, or too ill, who perhaps hates Hitler but has had no opportunity to show it in accordance with category 19, who is not skilled, nor can enlist in the Pioneer Corps because he may be ill or has lost three fingers at work, who has a son in the Army but who is not British, is a decent man and a true citizen. The trader, the business-man, the artisan and the clerk have no chance and no hope . . . .'

When Morrison's major statement on his internment policy finally came on 26 November, the case of this 'ordinary man' was on the way to solution. In the first place he made it abundantly clear that the government regarded enlistment in the Pioneer Corps as the appropriate method of obtaining release for men between the ages of eighteen and fifty. It was 'an opportunity clearly to demonstrate their friendliness to the Allied cause. . . . They should not therefore defer offering their services to the Corps in the expectation that there may be enlargements affecting them, of the existing categories set out in the White Paper.' A week later he punched this point home, reminding such men 'that compulsory military service applies to British subjects'.

But, for men who did not qualify for the Pioneer Corps, because of their age or their physical condition, Morrison introduced a new category into the White Paper, giving them the opportunity to obtain their release if they could satisfy a tribunal that they were opposed to the Nazi or Fascist systems, that they were positively friendly towards the Allied cause and that they would remain steadfast towards that cause in all circumstances.

By 3 December approximately 8000 German, Austrian and Italian internees had been released, leaving some 19,000 still in camps in Britain, Canada and Australia. Of the 8000 released, 1273 were men who had applied satisfactorily under category 12 for entry to the Pioneer Corps. It was the second largest category, only exceeded at this stage by category 3, the invalid and infirm.

From the issue of the first White Paper on 31 July, posters explaining and encouraging enlistment in the Corps had been displayed in all the male camps. They had met a mixed response.

'Eventually it became clear', writes Erich Mark, 'that we had two basic options: wait for Parliament or join the Army. My conception of what joining the Army was all about was of the haziest – I did not feel cut out for the life of a soldier and thought I might not even pass the medical test. However, better to try than to wait still longer, as it was then September and the Battle of Britain appeared to have been won. I duly signed a form, was given a distinctly cursory medical, declared to be A1, short-sightedness notwithstanding, and, although I did not get into the first release batch, left Douglas with the second, some time in October.'

Kurt felt differently: 'The Pioneer Corps was a sore point. After the horrible events, separation, broken promise, what state would Freda be in? I could not go, could I? I said I could not join yet, not under duress, not behind barbed wire. Once free, I might decide. We were the original fighters against Hitler. Besides, we still had relatives in Germany.'

From the date of Morrison's statement, the feeling in the House of Commons gradually became markedly less critical of government internment policy, and the tempo of releases accelerated. Not all of them, of course, were in connection with the Pioneer Corps. Not Henry Prais: 'I got out in December. When Anderson published his famous "points", his categories for release, I came under war work. I wrote to the farmer whom I had worked for outside Glasgow and he applied for my release. I was released and I returned to his farm. I had to register with the police in Glasgow, who crossed out "German" in my registration book, and wrote in "stateless". I applied for release to get out of that useless existence and do something for the war effort. Otherwise, it was the craziest holiday I have ever had.'

Chaim Rabin's 'war work' was of a different nature: 'I got out on the basis of important war work. It was very liberally interpreted in my case. Professor Margoliouth had died and had left his library to the Oriental Institute. They wanted me to catalogue it. I was invited by the University of Oxford as an Arabist. They thought it would take me two months. It actually took six. I have a great suspicion that the government wanted to get us out.'

Complaints of conditions inside the camps were also dying down, and reports of improvements coming to the fore. Osbert Peake told the House on 3 December that in an Isle of Man internment-camp a watch-repairing industry had been established, which was even undertaking repairs for London firms. The boots and shoes of the women internees at Port St Mary were being taken to the men's camp for repair by experienced cobblers. 600 men were going out daily to engage in agricultural work. And the Home Office had sent a welfare officer to co-ordinate welfare activities and try and increase the scope of employment still further.

When Rabbi Dr S. Schonfeld conducted his fourth tour of the camps, he too noted progress. The releases meant that there was no longer overcrowding and the sharing by two men of one double bed had almost completely disappeared. There were regular walks outside the camp in which some 400 men joined, and in good weather the inmates of Sefton camp were allowed on the sands at low tide. Each camp had a welfare fund, derived from profits on canteen sales and other sources, which was used to assist the destitute. Radios were available in some camps, bought out of contributions by internees, while in Hutchinson there were loud-speakers in every house which relayed BBC programmes, as well as talks, entertainment and English lessons from the camp's own studio. The wiring, installation and broadcasts were the work of the internees themselves. Music was encouraged in all the camps; Sefton had ten pianos. At Onchan internees paid regular visits to the local cinema. Camp magazines were produced.

Most significant as far as this particular visitor was concerned, Jewish High Holy Day services had been held everywhere, and a number of *Succoth* [tabernacles] erected in each camp. Two kosher hotels were functioning: the Breakwater at Port Erin and the Ballaqueeney at Port St Mary. The first Jewish burial ground in the Isle of Man had been consecrated in November.

Christian festivals were not neglected. Dr H. reports, 'We celebrated a quite happy Christmas at the Hydro, with good food, and everybody received a little present, which the commandant allowed me to buy at Douglas with another internee. We did our shopping, as far as I can remember, at Woolworth's and returned with a large sack of small presents.'

More good news was to come. On 12 November, Osbert Peake had said that the government wanted male internees to make up their minds about volunteering for the Pioneer Corps before it made a definite announcement about the establishment of mixed camps. On 21 January 1941, he gave the first practical details of a scheme to make them a reality. Enquiries he had been conducting showed that the best way of carrying out the project was to assign married couples accommodation in one of the two villages used for the women's camps. The committee reviewing the cases of female internees had made such good progress, and so many women had in consequence been released, that it should be possible in the near future to house the remaining women in one village and utilise the other for husbands and wives whose release could not be authorised.

Marie Neurath did not stay to see the mixed camp. She and Otto were released on 8 February, on the basis of an invitation to Otto to lecture at All Souls' College, Oxford. Marie did not lose contact with Port Erin, and letters from the husband of the proprietress of her former hotel kept her in touch with developments.

Port Erin,
17 February 1941.

Dear Marie,
(I'm sure you will not resent the familiarity now that you have moved from 'those people' to these.) . . .

Everyone here is delighted that yourself and Dr Neurath have ceased to be the sport of Fate or the Warmakers or what you will and are now in a position to settle down and resume a valuable existence. I need not add that in the 'Everyone here' I am included. . . . Alas!, Marie, there's an element of melancholy in the departure of all the fine folks one has known for so many months.

I don't know whether the fact may be attributed to the power of your propaganda in *Turandot* but the mixed camp is now an actuality and will commence almost at once.

The weather is nothing like so 'caald' as formerly but fires continue to be requested and – after the usual arguments – granted . . . .

Events continue at the tempo you knew (and all fretted under) for so many months. The releases seem to have slowed down a little as only a third of your number left last week. . . .

Port Erin,
31 March 1941

Dear Old 'Kaliph',
Yours of the 27th arrived this afternoon and created a pleasant diversion in what has come to be rather a monotonous existence. The outgoings of the last few weeks have left the place very flat indeed. We, ourselves, have only eight left. . . .

I suppose the idea will have some amusement for you, Mary, but the fact is I have regretful moods, often, about the departure of 'You People' – moods, perhaps, best described in that song, so popular here, 'The Kerry Dance'. After all, the experience was, for me, quite unique. It is not often that a sober-minded individual like myself finds himself in the company of so much diversified femininity – in abnormal circumstances at that! A rather high percentage of which femininity being educated and cultured beyond the average standard of most of the women I come in contact with normally.

Whatever happens I shall not forget the 'session' 1940–41. I have retained innumerable impressions. . . .

The mixed camp commences in a fortnight's time – official!

The mixed camp finally got off the ground. 'It was perfection', an internee told me. 'I had no worries: I had my husband: the food was very good. It was an absolute holiday, paid for by His Majesty's Government.'

Freda also sampled these delights. 'They said if the mixed camp came it would be behind barbed wire; did we really want that? Yes, we did. If we could live together, we would live in a cellar.

'When it came we each had a room in this big hotel. We earned 7s. 6d. a week for washing up 760 dishes after meals. There were about 400–500 people in the hotel [the Ballaqueeney]. That's when we made friends. One lot of friends who owned a factory got enormous parcels of food from their family. My eyes nearly popped out of my head. Other friends had no children and every party had to be in their room. We also had a frying-pan and we used to fry bacon. People from the kosher side of the house came looking to see what was happening. One side of the dining-room was kosher and one side was liberal. Naturally, there were problems which had to be solved amicably, in such a mixed assembly, thrown together by such tragic events. And, of course, they were heated at times. They accused us of using their cloths and mixing up their things. There were separate washing-up arrangements for the kosher. One of our people took over the cooking. He cooked beautifully with the same rations.

'There were several professional theatre people there, producers and so on. We produced a revue, plays, Shakespeare. I took part in the theatrical productions. I was a photographer in the revue. It was most beautifully done and there were some lovely tunes. Everything was composed and written there. It was all in German. This was not so good, because when we came to Leicester we were not fluent in English. Evie only spoke German. There was a lot of cultural life going on. We really got going with the classes.

'Kurt worked in the cobblers' shop. He used to take Evie along and the pram stood outside the shop. We also made string bags; the camp commandant sold them. You got about sixpence a dozen. We were allowed to go to the cinema and to go shopping, but we were always accompanied by a guard. We could use the beach and we went swimming in the summer – in fact, practically all the year round. Every morning we had gym from seven to eight o'clock – a woman took that – and after it we went swimming. We were all very fit. The only trouble with the baby was that she did not get enough vegetables and lived mainly on milk and semolina. She got very fat.

'When the news was on every night, everyone was shouting, "Quiet! Quiet!" We heard the news about deportations from Holland and Germany. We had Red Cross letters from Holland and they received one or two letters from us. There was tension all the time: "Will my case come up for release?" We felt we were wasting time there. We wanted to make a start. We would have enjoyed it more if it had not been for this feeling. And also not knowing what was happening in Holland.

'In the end our case came up for release, and then the moment arrived. Our friends had gone to Leicester about ten months before. They wrote every week and sent a parcel once a month. In August 1942 we left the isle, watched by a warden, *en route* to Leicester via Fleetwood, starting auxiliary war work. Then life began in earnest.'

That some of the interned women were able to participate in the mixed camp was the consequence of progress in another direction: the return of their husbands from Canada. Already in December 1940, the release of ninety-four internees in Canada had been authorised. By 22 January 1941, 107 volunteers for the Pioneer Corps and 131 internees who appeared to be eligible for release under the categories of the White Paper were back in Britain. In addition Morrison announced that he had specifically authorised the release of fifty-one other internees in Canada and these men had also been sent back.

Despite the stringent Canadian immigration laws, some internees succeeded in staying in Canada; Leon Feldman, for example; or Martin Ostwald: 'Fairly soon after we arrived, anyone could go back to England to join the Pioneer Corps. I was going to do this and then I learned that the Pioneer Corps was not fighting; it was just digging in the rubble of London. I found that degrading. Some people did that; others had *proteczia* [influence]. I hoped that the Canadian army would eventually take us as full citizens, but this did not happen.

'The Pioneer Corps was the only way of getting back to England. Most of us decided to sit it out and wait for Canada to release us. Then Canada entered the war. There was a shortage of farm labour and anyone willing to go on a farm as a labourer could go. I was involved in the camp school; I was assistant principal – people took Matric in the camp.

'The Canadian optical industry was at the time monopolised by a Jew, who jumped into the breach and said that anyone willing to do lens-grinding, he would find a job for. As this was a war industry, the Canadians let them out.

'Some of us wanted very badly to go to university. A clever lawyer from the Canadian Jewish Congress found sponsors for us to guarantee us morally and financially. The Canadian government initially did not want to let us out in Canada because there was a law that an immigrant to Canada had to arrive on public transport. But our lawyer found that this did not apply to students. Therefore they agreed to let us out provided a sponsor, guaranteeing our moral integrity and assuming financial responsibility for us, could be found.

'I was released in 1942. This was a great time for us. For two years I had not seen a female or an ordinary street or shop. The immigration officer came to the camp and gave us identity papers and a visa and arrangements were made for us to go on a train.'

The unravelling process took rather longer to get going in Australia. By 18 December the release of only thirty-seven internees had been authorised; by 6 February 1941 the figure had risen to a mere 170. And only on 21 January had Peake been able to inform the House of Commons that the Australian authorities had agreed to allow Britain to send out a representative to fulfil the task, analogous to Paterson's in Canada, of expediting the procedure for dealing with the cases of the internees who appeared to be eligible for release under the White Paper, including those who desired to emigrate or to enlist in the Pioneer Corps.

Klaus Loewald remembers the call to arms: 'The Liaison Officer, Major Julian Layton, whom the British government sent to Australia in early 1941, brought important news. Those of us in both camps who were ready and willing to join the British Army were to return to England at short notice. All of us were to submit applications for release. Those who obtained it and wished to return without joining the Army were to be permitted to do so if and when shipping space became available and upon a written "willingness to travel" which renounced claims to specific itineraries and to fresh food *en route*. All those who had suffered losses on board the *Dunera* were allowed to submit claims for financial restitution. On the supposition, justified as it turned out, that the number of Army recruits would be large, the camps at Hay were to be evacuated and the remaining internees to move to a camp in northern Victoria, near Tatura. . . .

'In response to the call to arms, about 1000 internees from both camps left Hay in early May. . . . The farewell my camp gave to the departing soldiers-to-be was proud and sad; those who remained watched with apprehension as 500 of our best, young and hopeful comrades marched out joyfully and erect, away from the community which they had adorned for the previous nine months, towards the railway-station and an uncertain fate. . . .

'As the camp faced its total abandonment, it now presented the aspect of a half-deserted town. Rumours began to circulate that prisoners of war were to be its next inhabitants. This caused us to decide that we would not bequeath to them such comforts as we had been able to provide for ourselves during the preceding months. We built a large mountain of chairs, benches, tables and other items, crowned it with an effigy on which we fastened a pin with a swastika, and on the eve of our departure made a bonfire of these possessions, which burned all night. A friend of mine helped enliven the spectacle by persuading one of our more exhibitionist colleagues to perform a naked veil-dance round the conflagration. The next morning we left for Orange and Tatura.'

The internees had been given the choice of going straight to Tatura, or of spending two months in a camp in Orange on the way. Rudi Guttman went to Tatura.

'It was a much nicer place, not out in the desert (Hay had been desert – not a tree in sight). We were not there long. We (the people who wanted to go back to England) were moved to Barmera in South Australia. There I got a job in charge of a survey party setting up a new camp for German prisoners of war – who in the event never came. The Australian guards there were very puzzled by their English-speaking prisoners. After that, I got the most exciting job: I drove the shit-house express. We had very primitive toilets, just planks with buckets beneath them. The buckets were collected once a day and emptied into urns and loaded on to a wagon drawn by two sturdy horses. The horses were driven by me. I went into the bush with the urns and drums of water, emptied the urns into a hole, washed them out with the water and drove back. It was a very good job; I enjoyed that.

'When I think about it in retrospect, the people in prisoner-of-war camps were much worse off. We had no problems with our guards and we had good food. But we did not know why we were there. We had no thought of escape; we wanted to get out legally. Then we were given the opportunity . . . .'

So was Jakob Felsenstein: 'By very early July 1941, I joined a transport for the return journey. There had been a bigger transport before then, but I had been in two minds whether to risk a transatlantic journey in wartime. That was why I joined this small transport with only eleven men.

'On the freighter we spent our time pleasantly, mainly on deck with the usual deck sports. Food was plentiful; I even managed very well on fish, eggs, butter, etc. We then anchored at Baltimore. The other passengers were allowed on shore, but not ex-internees. We proceeded to the Canadian port of Halifax, where we had to wait several days until a convoy was put together; ours was the largest convoy, with over sixty ships. The size and number of the ships and the smoke from all their funnels in the evening sunset was most beautiful. The journey was slow as we had to adjust ourselves to the speed of the slowest of the boats. Eventually, we arrived at Belfast . . . .'

Rudi Guttman came back towards the end of 1941: 'One day we were put on a train and taken to Sydney. There, we were put in a camp near the harbour. Shops brought their goods to us there and brought all sorts of things. We looked like vagabonds. We were given slacks and a jacket, a couple of shirts, underwear, socks and shoes. Then one day we were marched onto a ship. There was no barbed wire; this was a pleasant change. But there was another surprise: after the ship left Sydney, it went to Auckland. It was there five days, but we were not let off the ship – and the Jewish community there had invited us! Not being let off at Auckland made me madder than the whole internment: I was on my way to fight for "King and country"!

'We came home through Panama and landed at Liverpool. I had heard while I was in camp that my father had died following an operation. I heard later that my mother had been deported; I had a letter from the Red Cross.

'At Liverpool we were taken straight to an induction centre, went through a medical and given the famous AB64 [soldier's pay book], a uniform and outfit. Then we were sent on leave. It was the first time for eighteen months that I was a comparatively free agent. I went to London and then to my school because it was the only home I had.'

# Epilogue

Releases from internment now proceeded apace. By March 1941, 12,500 people had been freed; by April, 14,250; by August, 17,745. In the summer of 1942 fewer than 5000 enemy aliens remained in the Isle of Man. Of these, according to the Board of Deputies of British Jews, only 300–400 were refugees.

The vast majority who had been released began yet again to rebuild shattered lives, some of them with remarkable success.

For some, such as Klaus Loewald, the experience of internment had been a valuable one: 'To me, the two years had passed very quickly. Many windows had been opened in my mind, and I was conscious of having obtained the kind of education which attendance at school could not provide. My years of internment constituted a period of uninterrupted good fortune. I had entered them in a spirit of irresponsible youthful adventure, and at their end I had to remind myself that it was not wisdom which had guided my steps.'

Few retain the bitterness of the internee who wrote to me from America: 'The Germans overran France, and the English government was in a panic and had to show their people that they were on the alert. So they arrested friendly refugees and sent many of them by boats to Canada. When at the same time thousands of English citizens belonged to the Mosley party and were waiting for Adolf Hitler to invade England. It was the biggest farce and one of the most cowardly steps the English government took against the refugees.'

For some, internment had changed the course of their lives. 'If they hadn't interned me,' said Felix Darnbacher, 'I would not have come to Israel. I would have been so British.'

Others are so British. Eugen Glueckauf writes, 'A year after my release I got the offer of a McKinnon Research Studentship of the Royal Society which ran for two years, and I continued to do meteorological war research on the water content of the stratosphere. In 1944 I applied for a position with the Department of

175

Scientific and Industrial Research, involving research on the separation of isotopes, in collaboration with Sir Francis Simon, who was Professor of Physics at Oxford. The work was to be done at Durham. After getting naturalised in 1946 I applied for a post with the Atomic Energy Research Establishment at Harwell, and we moved there in 1947. This proved to be a most important change of status. Though only recently naturalised I was accepted without reservations as a Principal Scientific Officer, and in due course was promoted to Deputy Chief Scientist and Head of the Physical and Radio-Chemistry branch. In spite of an audible accent, I assimilated well, was elected a Fellow of the Royal Society, and was elected and served for more than twenty years on our local parish council.

'It goes without saying that I never felt any resentment about the few months I spent in internment. My years as a British subject were the best I could have wished for, and this country has become our home.'

'Others take a philosophical approach. 'When I was released', Henry Prais told me, 'I had to fill in a form giving my past record. Had you ever been in prison before? November–December 1938: Buchenwald, on the charge of being a Jew; July–December 1940: Onchan, on the charge of being a German.

'From 1936 onwards you had become so accustomed to an insecure existence that you did not find injustice surprising. You were conditioned to the fact that life was going to be insecure from then on. The only thing that you felt bad about: for the Nazis to call you a Jew – well, that was all right. For the British to call you a German, that was unfair. But we used to say, "The poor buggers don't know any better." You made excuses for them. The Jews always say, "Perhaps we are to blame." '

'I hold no resentment', Dr H. writes. 'The rounding-up happened in the panic of Dunkirk and, in spite of all the sufferings and inconveniences, we must not forget that we lived on the Isle of Man during the time of the worst bombing, which we (and later the children) were spared. How many people who were sent to concentration camps would have been happy to suffer the hardships of internment? Nevertheless it was at that time hard to understand that one had been classed with obvious Nazis, from whom one had tried to escape.'

'Now we understand it, of course,' Freda explains, 'but at the time we only thought, "Why did they do this to us?" '

# Bibliography

Peter and Leni Gillman, *'Collar the Lot!'* (London, 1980).
'Judex', *Anderson's Prisoners* (London, 1940).
Francis Lafitte, *The Internment of Aliens* (London, 1940).
Benzion Patkin, *The Dunera Internees* (Australia, 1979).
Ronald Stent, *A Bespattered Page?* (London, 1980).
Austin Stevens, *The Dispossessed* (London, 1975).
Eugen Spier, *The Protecting Power* (London, 1951).
Bernard Wasserstein, *Britain and the Jews of Europe, 1939–45* (London, 1979).
John W. Wheeler-Bennett, *John Anderson, Viscount Waverley* (London, 1962).

# Index